Reader's Digest
Tools &
Techniques
DIY Manual

Reader's Digest
Tools &
Techniques
DIY Manual

Expert guidance on choosing and using DIY equipment

Published by
The Reader's Digest Association Limited
London • New York • Sydney • Montreal

Contents

Introduction

Basic tools

Basic skills

Decorating your home

Improvements & maintenance

About this book

With the correct tools and some basic skills, making improvements or undertaking repairs can save money and help to transform your home. From establishing a basic tool kit to mastering techniques such as tiling a wall or unblocking a pipe, this book offers simple, practical advice, technical know-how and clear step-by-step guidance that you can apply to numerous tasks and projects around your home.

With the average cost of moving house in the UK approaching £10,000, and plumbers typically charging from £30–£50 for the first hour's work, it makes sense to acquire the tools and techniques that will enable you to tackle a whole range of tasks around your home yourself.

On pages 10–16 you will find the advice you need to equip yourself with a basic tool kit. Many are essential tools that no home should be without; they will enable you to undertake those everyday DIY jobs that all householders have to face. The following pages feature specialist tools for specific jobs, advice on fixtures and fittings, and easy-to-follow instructions on decorating and maintenance to help you make the most of your home.

Filling your tool box

Armed with a sturdy tool box, Chapter One details the various tools with which you should fill it. Once you have acquired general-purpose essentials such as a claw hammer, pliers and a set of screwdrivers, there is information on tools for more specialist tasks, such as measuring and marking, holding and gripping, power tools, and other useful items. If you are planning to invest in a cordless drill, turn to page 25 to find out more about the accessories you can add that will allow you to use it for a range of other jobs – including sanding attachments and polishing pads.

Pages 17–19 list the range of woodworking tools that can be built up slowly to complement your basic tool kit. It's also a good idea to keep a supply of nails, screws and wall fixings in your DIY kit, and pages 20–24 are filled with helpful advice on what to keep in stock and on choosing wall fixings appropriate to the job in hand, whether that's erecting shelving or putting up a curtain rail.

Mastering the basic skills

Many DIY jobs that will need to be undertaken around your home rely on a few basic skills. Chapter Two identifies the tools you will need for these jobs and explains how to use them.

One of the first steps in many projects is sizing up: measuring, positioning and locating concealed hazards, and pages 28–29 show you how. Few DIY jobs do not involve drilling holes at some point, so there is advice on getting to know your drill, on pages 33–34, and using screws to secure items to surfaces such as wood, metal, plastic as well as walls and ceilings (pages 31–32).

If you need to change the washer on a leaky tap or remove old wallplugs, gripping and tightening skills explained on pages 36–37 will make the task seem simple. Splits in woodwork or cracks in plaster will need making good – or restoring to their original state. From page 41, there is advice on all the skills you will need for repairing and filling wood, plaster and problem gaps, such as around window frames, like a professional.

Finally, pages 47–69, deal with wood. From choosing and buying to measuring and marking, cutting wood or boards, smoothing and shaping, to using a router, making basic joints and information on assembling flat-pack furniture.

Transforming your home

The most popular DIY project in Britain is painting and decorating. A new colour scheme can transform the appearance of

your home and need not be expensive if you can avoid employing professionals to do the work. There is now a huge variety of tools available in DIY stores and, if you choose the right ones, they will make the jobs you plan faster and easier.

Chapter Three provides advice on the tools you will need for preparation, painting, wallpapering and tiling, pages 72–78, and offers guidance on the all-important preparatory stages of a project on pages 79–83. This includes stripping wallpaper or paint – including using a steam stripper or hot-air gun – and filling small cracks and holes.

Then, on pages 84–89, our experts will show you the correct techniques for painting, whether you are applying primers, undercoat or topcoats, including gloss and varnish. There is instruction on using a brush, roller or paint pad, and tips on painting a wall or ceiling as well as different surfaces, such as bare plaster, paper, textured coatings, woodwork or ceiling tiles.

The final section suggests the best methods for looking after your equipment, so that you can save even more money by using your brushes and rollers time and time again.

Wallpapering can bring about a dramatic change to a room, but it is surprisingly quick and easy to do once you have mastered the basic techniques. On pages 90–96, these techniques are explained and illustrated, from hanging standard wallpaper to papering in awkward places – for example around light switches or sockets, behind a radiator or around a recessed window.

And to add the finishing touches to kitchens and bathrooms, pages 97–103 show you all you need to know to position, cut, fix and grout tiles with expert results every time.

Repairs and improvements

If you are undertaking improvements, Chapter 4 gives you the know-how to do it without the help of the professionals, from sanding floors to lifting boards to access pipes or cables beneath, and from hanging doors to patching damaged plaster.

While there are jobs that do require a professional, such as work involving the gas supply or installing new lights or power sockets, there are many others that you can tackle yourself. Once you've read these pages, clearing a blocked sink or draining down the hot or cold water system need never faze you again.

Equipped with the knowledge of how to bend and join pipes (pages 114–120), you can undertake any number of plumbing tasks, such as installing a washing machine or moving a wash basin. And pages 121–124 detail the essential wiring techniques of preparing cables and making safe electrical connections so that you can replace damaged fittings or rewire a plug with confidence.

Basic tools

The basic tool kit

These are the tools you will need to tackle most of the common DIY jobs you are likely to face as a householder. Some are essentials that no home should be without, while others can be bought as and when you need them. The tools you will need for woodworking are detailed from page 17.

General purpose tools

The tool box

You will need a sturdy tool box in which to store your small hand tools. Many sizes and styles are available; to start with, pick a light but sturdy plastic case with a lift-out tray for small tools. You can always buy a second or a bigger box as your tool kit grows. Avoid metal tool boxes; they are heavy to carry around and they rust.

Tool box

Claw hammer

Pincers   Pliers

Nail punch

Tenon saw

Trimming knife

Filling knife

Junior hacksaw

Ball-pein hammer

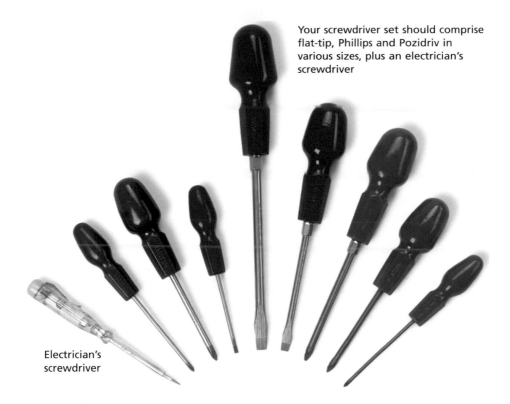

Your screwdriver set should comprise flat-tip, Phillips and Pozidriv in various sizes, plus an electrician's screwdriver

Electrician's screwdriver

Pincers

Looking more like an instrument of torture than a DIY tool, pincers are extremely useful jacks of all trades. They are designed primarily for pulling out unwanted pins, tacks and nails – from floorboards, for example – but can also be put to other tasks, such as pulling out picture hooks without damaging the plaster or nibbling awkward shapes out of ceramic tiles. Pincers are usually about 200mm long and are inexpensive to buy.

Pliers

A pair of combination pliers is another multi-purpose tool that is well worth having in your tool kit. Their serrated jaws are useful for gripping all sorts of things, such as the wire loop that holds the bath plug on its chain, the corroded piston on a faulty ballvalve or the shattered remains of a light bulb stuck in its lampholder. You can use them as a makeshift spanner if none is to hand. You can twist and cut wire, and straighten bent metal. Basic pliers have metal handles; if comfort in use is important to you, buy electrician's pliers with insulated plastic handles instead.

Trimming knife

A trimming knife with replaceable blades is a DIY essential. A standard blade will cut paper, card and thin sheet materials such as

plasterboard, and will mark clear cutting lines on all sorts of surfaces. Fitted with special blades, the knife can cut sheet flooring, plastic laminates, even wood and metal. Knives are available with fixed blades (initially covered by a slip-on blade guard, which is often lost), or with retractable blades that are safer to use and to carry around. Most knives allow you to store spare blades (except long wood and metal-cutting ones) inside the knife handle. Make sure you have plenty of spares.

Hacksaw

Hacksaws are designed to cut metal and take replaceable blades. You might need one to cut through a rusty nail or bolt, or an unwanted pipe. A hacksaw will also cut through plastic – a curtain rail, for example – and can even be used for cutting small pieces of wood, such as timber mouldings. For all these jobs, an inexpensive junior hacksaw is ideal. It takes slim, 150mm long blades, which are held in tension by the spring of the one-piece steel frame. Buy a pack of spare blades, too.

Screwdrivers

Within reason, you can never have too many screwdrivers. Screws come with head recesses of different types, ranging from straight slots to cross and hexagon shapes, and in different sizes.

To start with, you need a flat-tip screwdriver with a blade about 125mm long for slotted-head screws, and a No. 2 Phillips cross-tip screwdriver that will also drive other types of cross-head screws, such as Pozidriv and Prodrive.

You will also need a small electrician's screwdriver for fiddly jobs. This has an insulated handle, for safety's sake.

If you need more screwdrivers, it is worth looking out for screwdriver sets sold in a storage case. These typically include two or three drivers for slotted-head screws, plus Phillips and Pozidriv drivers in two sizes for large and small cross-head screws of different types. The set may have a master handle, into which you slot the blade you need for the task. This type of set saves space but can be fiddly to use if you have a complicated project in hand.

Saws

If you plan to cut any wood larger than a slim moulding (which your junior hacksaw will deal with), you need a proper saw. Invest in a tenon saw, which has a rectangular blade about 250mm long stiffened along the top with a strip of brass or steel. The handle is either wood or moulded plastic. As its name implies, the tenon saw is designed primarily for cutting woodworking joints but it will cope with all sorts of other minor woodwork jobs, such as trimming wall battens or cutting a shelf to length. The thickness of timber it will cut is limited by the depth of the blade.

Hammers

The most versatile hammer to have is a claw hammer, which will drive all but the smallest pins and can also be used to lever out old nails by fitting the grooved claw under the nail head. Choose one with a metal or glass-fibre shaft and a rubber grip, with a head weighing 16oz or 20oz (hammers still come in imperial sizes).

To accompany your claw hammer, you will need to buy a nail punch (also known as a nail set). This is a small steel tool about 100mm long, with a knurled shaft and a tapered point. It is used with a hammer to drive nail heads below the wood surface, preventing the hammer head from striking and denting the wood. They are also essential when you are sanding floorboards, for example, as protruding nails will rip the sanding discs on the sander.

Add a small pin hammer and ball-pein hammer to your tool kit if you drive a lot of small nails and panel pins. They will have wooden handles and lightweight heads.

Filling knife

This tool has a wood or plastic handle and a flexible steel blade, and is used for applying filler to holes and defects in wood or plaster. Buy a 25mm and a 50mm knife for everyday use. Do not confuse a filling knife with a stripping knife, which has a stiffer blade (see page 72).

Measuring and marking

Straightedge

A long steel or aluminium straightedge is essential for many DIY jobs, from checking the flatness of surfaces (a tiled wall, for example) to guiding a trimming knife when cutting such things as vinyl flooring. Buy one 1m long for maximum usefulness, with both metric and imperial markings along it.

Straightedge

Spirit levels

Tape measure

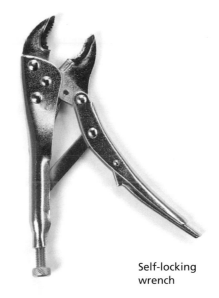

Self-locking
wrench

Adjustable
spanners

Tape measure

You will need a steel tape measure for measuring and estimating jobs. An ideal size is a 5m tape, which will cope with measuring up a room as well as taking smaller measurements. Most have metric and imperial markings, so you can also use the tape as a handy conversion device.

Choose a tape measure with a locking device that keeps the tape, or blade, extended while you use it and note down the measurements.

Spirit level

This tool is essential when you are putting up such things as shelves and curtain tracks to ensure that you get them absolutely level. It is also crucial for checking anything that needs to be truly vertical.

A spirit level is a plastic or alloy bar with vials containing an air bubble set into the long edge and usually also at each end. The level is horizontal or vertical when the bubble is exactly centred between the marks on the appropriate vial. Some have adjustable vials that rotate to allow you to check a specific angle.

For accuracy and longevity, buy a metal one that is at least 300mm long. To check levels over longer distances, balance the spirit level on a timber straightedge. Take care of your spirit levels, as dents and other damage will make them inaccurate.

Holding and gripping

Self-locking wrench

This versatile tool, commonly known as a Mole wrench from the name of the original manufacturer, can be used like a pair of pliers or as a makeshift extra spanner. Its wide serrated jaws will grip round things such as the knurled nuts on waste traps, and its lockable jaws mean that you can also use it as a clamp when you need an extra pair of hands.

Spanners

Spanners are better at turning nuts and bolts than pliers, and you will probably have to undo something that's bolted together or tighten a leaky plumbing fitting sooner or later. What you need is an adjustable spanner with a jaw opening up to about 30mm – this will be big enough to grip the nuts on plumbing fittings, yet capable of tackling smaller nuts. too. The so-called crescent pattern with its offset head is best at getting into awkward positions. It is a good idea to buy a pair of adjustable spanners as you will often need more than one at a time.

Power tools

Jigsaw

A jigsaw is one of the most useful of all power tools. Even if you do not do much woodwork, you can justify its purchase for its all-round versatility. It has a relatively short blade that protrudes from the baseplate of the saw, and this cuts on the upstroke. Because of the thinness of the blade, you can make curved cuts with it as well as straight ones, simply by driving the saw blade along a marked cutting line. You can also make cuts away from the edge of the workpiece – to fit a letterbox in a front door, for example, or make a cut-out in a worktop for an inset sink or hob.

Although the jigsaw is primarily designed for cutting wood and man-made boards, it will also cut materials such as metal, rigid plastic and ceramic tiles as long as the correct type of blade is fitted.

Features to look out for when choosing a jigsaw are adequate power (at least 500 watts), variable speed, a dust bag or vacuum cleaner attachment to help to collect dust, and a blade fitting arrangement that does not need tools. Keep a stock of standard wood-cutting blades for general work, and buy specialist blades only when you need them.

Cordless jigsaws are available but they are comparatively expensive and probably not worth the cost unless you plan to do a lot of cutting far from a power source.

Sander

Finishing new wood, keying the surface of paintwork before redecorating it and removing surplus material such as plaster filler are all jobs that require sanding – using an abrasive paper to create a smooth surface. You can do the job by hand, but for all but the smallest areas this is one of the most tedious and time-consuming DIY jobs. A power sander does all the work in a fraction of the time, and even gathers up the dust if you buy the right type.

Power sanders come in more varieties than any other tool, ranging from tiny hand-sized finishing sanders to high-powered belt sanders. There are even sanders with interchangeable heads for sanding awkward areas. As a first choice for general smoothing work, an eccentric or random-orbit sander is probably the best. This combines the fine finish of an orbital sander with the fast stock removal of a disc sander, and can be fitted with a wide range of abrasive sheets.

Most random-orbit sanders take circular sanding discs 115mm or 125mm in diameter. You attach the discs to the baseplate with touch-and-close (Velcro) fastenings. Holes in the discs line up with holes in the baseplate through which the sander's motor extracts dust, either depositing it in a small dust bag or delivering it via a hose connection to a vacuum cleaner.

Jigsaw

Sander

Flat wood drill bits

Screwdriver bits for drill

Cordless drill

Countersink drill bit

Twist drill bits

Masonry drill bits

Drill

You will need a power drill for all sorts of DIY jobs. The most versatile choice is a cordless drill, which has a rechargeable battery and can be used anywhere without the need for a power supply. Cordless drills are not as powerful as mains-powered models, and can be more expensive. However, they double up as a power screwdriver thanks to their low chuck speed, and their reverse gear allows you to undo screws as well. A model with hammer action will drill holes in all but the hardest walls. Battery sizes range from 9.6V (volts) up to a massive 24V; a drill rated at 14.4 or 18V will be powerful enough to cope with almost every job. Choose one that is comfortable and well-balanced to hold, and is not too heavy to handle easily. Keep a spare battery, so that one can be kept fully charged while the other is in use.

Drill bits

Your cordless drill will need a range of drill bits for the various jobs it can do. All these bits can be purchased individually, but if you do a lot of different DIY jobs, it may be more economical to buy a mixed set in a special storage box or case.

Twist drill bits make small holes in wood, man-made boards and metal. These are likely to be your most-used bits and it is worth investing in a good set. Buy a set of HSS (high-speed steel) drill bits containing sizes up to 10mm, stored in a metal case that will last longer than a plastic one. Carbon steel bits are cheaper than HSS ones, but become blunt more quickly.

Flat wood bits drill larger holes in wood and boards, and come in sizes from 12mm up to 38mm. Buy them as and when you need them and store them in their packaging – usually a plastic sleeve.

Masonry drill bits make holes in solid walls, usually to take wallplugs when making wall fixings. There is no need to buy a boxed set, which will contain many sizes of drill bit you will never use. Instead, match the sizes you buy to the wallplugs and other fixings you usually use – probably 6, 7 and 8mm. You may need longer and larger drill bits to make holes in walls for pipes and cables; buy them as and when you need them. Store them all in a tray in your tool box.

Screwdriver bits enable you to drive and remove screws using your cordless drill as a power screwdriver. One two-ended bit will probably be supplied with your drill; add a set containing bits for slotted-head, Phillips, Pozidriv and Torx screws.

Countersink bits make cone-shaped recesses in wood or metal to accept the heads of countersunk screws. Use them after you have drilled the hole to take the screw through the workpiece, carefully centring the countersink bit on the screw hole so that the screw sits neatly in place.

leaving one hand free to hold whatever you are fixing. You will also find it ideal for securing carpet underlay to floorboards, attaching fabric to roller blinds and even making small picture frames. The most versatile will fire staples of different sizes.

Work and access

Stepladders
A light but sturdy stepladder is essential if you are undertaking high-level work. Choose one that is versatile – some can be used in various combinations, for use in stairwells, for example – and has a grab rail and platform for resting tools or paint pots at the top. Make sure the feet have non-skid covers. Accessories such as clip-on trays, stand-offs (which keep the ladder away from the wall) and paint hooks are useful additions.

Workbench
The last essential for everyday DIY is a portable workbench. You can use it to support things while you cut, drill and assemble them, and its jaws will act as a large vice for gripping anything from a length of pipe to a room door. You can even stand on it at a pinch.
    Small basic types are surprisingly cheap; larger models cost more but may have extra features, such as dual height settings and movable jaws.

Other useful tools

Staple gun
The DIY version of the office stapler has all sorts of uses. It will fix webbing or fabric to furniture frames, trellis to fences and low-voltage wires to skirting boards, all the time

Cable and pipe detector
This small, battery-powered device detects the presence of electricity cable and plumbing pipes buried in the house walls. Some will also locate ceiling joists and the timber frame inside a partition wall, by detecting the line of fixing nails that holds the plasterboard cladding in place. Use it as a precaution to check for hidden pipes or cables before driving nails or drilling holes for wall fixings.

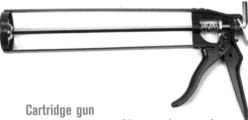

Cartridge gun
Many ready-to-use fillers, sealants and adhesives are now sold in standard-sized cartridges. To be able to use them, you need a cartridge gun. This inexpensive tool has an open metal or plastic frame that holds the cartridge, and is fitted with a simple trigger and piston mechanism that extrudes the contents of the cartridge as the trigger is squeezed. Cartridges come in two standard sizes, and you may need two gun sizes to take them.

Woodworking tools

These are the tools you will need if you plan to be more than an occasional weekend woodworker, cutting a wall batten to size or trimming the odd shelf to length. The list complements the basic tool kit described on pages 10–16, and can be built up tool-by-tool as your woodworking horizons expand.

Tools for marking

Marking gauge
This tool consists of a wooden beam with a hardened steel pin set into it near one end, and a wooden block that slides along the beam and can be secured to it with a thumbscrew.

The pin scribes a line at a fixed distance from the edge of the workpiece. It is used when marking out woodworking joints and is also useful for jobs such as centring locks on door edges and marking the depth of hinge recesses.

Mitre box
A three-sided, open-ended box with guide slots pre-cut in its opposite sides, used to guide a tenon saw blade when making 45° mitre cuts. The size of the box restricts the size of pieces that can be cut with it.

Try square and combination square
A try square has a rectangular metal blade fixed at 90° to a wooden, metal or plastic stock. It is an essential tool for marking a cutting line at right angles to the edge of a workpiece, and is also used for checking internal and external angles. A combination square is a variation on the theme, with a movable stock that can be used to mark 45° angles as well as right angles.

Sliding bevel
This is a sort of adjustable try square with a metal blade that can be set at any angle and locked in place with a wing nut. It is useful for fitting shelves in out-of-square alcoves or staircase balusters.

Tools for sawing

Circular saw
An essential if you plan to cut sheets of man-made boards, fit kitchen worktops or lay floorboards. It makes accurate, straight cuts and its tilting soleplate can be set to allow cuts at angles between 45° and 90°. A basic circular saw takes blades 150mm in diameter and has a maximum cutting depth of about 45mm. Semi-professional models take blades 190mm or 230mm in diameter, offering cutting depths of 65mm and 80mm at 90° and 45mm or 60mm at 45°. Some have a dust extraction facility.

Blades are available for fine cutting, cross cutting and rip cutting wood and man-made boards, and for cutting laminated chipboard kitchen worktops.

Coping saw
Designed for making curved cuts in wood and boards, it has a slim, replaceable blade mounted in a U-shaped steel frame with a

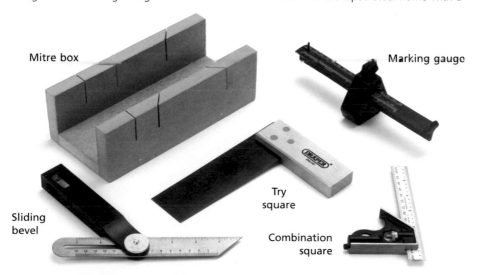

Mitre box

Marking gauge

Sliding bevel

Try square

Combination square

Circular saw

Coping saw

Panel saw

Hole saw and blade holder

Padsaw

Hole saw blades

with around 10 teeth per inch (tpi), fitted to a wooden or plastic handle. It is used mainly for cutting man-made boards by hand, and is a low-cost alternative to a circular saw. The blade may be PTFE-coated to minimise friction and the best saws have hard-point teeth that will stay sharp for longer. Fit the blade guard when storing.

Tools for shaping

Chisels
Chisels are essential for cutting many woodworking joints. They also chop out slots (mortises) for door locks, form recesses for hinges and do all sorts of general paring and shaping jobs. To start with, buy a set of bevel-edge chisels in 6, 12, 19 and 25mm sizes, ideally contained in a storage case. Keep the plastic blade guards on their tips when not in use. To keep the blades sharp, you will need an oilstone and some light machine oil. A honing guide will help you to sharpen them at the correct angle.

Mallet
This wooden hammer with a square, beechwood head is used mainly for striking chisel handles when cutting woodworking joints and for assembling joint components.

Planes and power planers
The bench plane is the traditional tool for reducing wood to the cross-sectional size wanted and finishing it with flat, smooth edges. It consists of a steel blade held at an angle to the tool's soleplate in an adjustable mount. The small block plane and larger smoothing plane are most widely used.

handle at one side. The frame holds the blade in tension and allows it to be rotated to prevent the frame from fouling the edge of the workpiece.

Hole saw
This attachment for a power drill is used to cut holes in wood and boards that are larger than the maximum size of a flat wood bit (around 38mm). The blade is a short length of saw formed into a cylinder and fitted into a blade holder. This carries a pilot drill at its centre that starts the hole and guides the saw blade into the wood. Sold in sets up to about 75mm in diameter.

Mitre saw
This useful tool consists of a framed saw with a fine-toothed blade mounted on guide bars over a steel base. The guide bars can be rotated to position the saw at any angle between 45° and 90° to the workpiece, which is clamped in place between the blade and the base while the cut is made. It is more accurate than a mitre box and can cut wider components.

Padsaw
The padsaw has a short, tapered blade fitted into a handle. It is used mainly for cutting holes in the centre of a workpiece, such as a keyhole in a door. You need a starter hole so you can insert the blade.

Panel saw
The panel saw has a plain steel blade usually about 560mm long, and typically

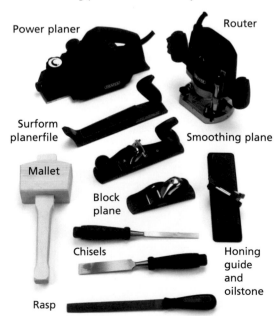

Power planer

Router

Surform planerfile

Smoothing plane

Mallet

Block plane

Chisels

Honing guide and oilstone

Rasp

The power planer does the work of a bench plane much more quickly. It has a rotating cylinder into which a replaceable cutting blade is fitted. It can remove up to 2–3mm of wood in each pass of the tool. It can also cut rebates when fitted with a detachable guide; the groove in its soleplate allows it to chamfer edges, too.

Router

A power tool with a motor that drives a cutter at very high speed. Straight cutters produce slots and grooves; shaped cutters create a wide range of edge mouldings. It is mounted on a baseplate on springs, allowing it to be 'plunged' into the work to a pre-set depth. Edge and circle guides allow the tool to follow the shape of the workpiece or to cut circular recesses. Many routers feature dust extraction and come with a few router bits. Extra bits can be bought as required.

Rasp

This tool is a coarse file used for shaping wood, especially curved surfaces. Buy a half-round rasp with one flat and one curved surface, which will shape convex and concave curves.

Surforms

The Surform range of shaping tools all have perforated blades that work like a miniature cheese grater, removing wood in a series of fine shavings. The range includes planes and files in several styles; the planerfile with its reversible handle is the most versatile. The blades are all replaceable when blunt.

Honing guide and oilstone

This wheeled guide holds a chisel or plane blade at the correct angle while it is being sharpened on an oilstone. It also holds it square to the surface of the stone. The oilstone is made of natural or synthetic abrasive material and usually has a fine and a coarse face; it is lubricated with light machine oil.

Workbench tools

Bench hook

This simple wooden bench aid is used to hold small workpieces, for example when cutting them to length. The hook is positioned on the workbench with the lower batten against its front edge. The workpiece is held against the upper batten.

Clamps

Clamps come in many styles and sizes, and have two main uses: holding workpieces securely on the workbench while they are cut, drilled or shaped; and clamping components such as woodworking joints together while the adhesive sets. G-clamps and screw clamps are traditional designs but fast-action trigger clamps and spring clamps are quicker and easier to use.

Drill stand

This bench aid clamps your power drill in an upright position, making it easy to drill perpendicular holes in the work surface. The running drill is moved up and down in the stand with a lever, and the depth of drilling can be pre-set to create stopped holes if required. Take your drill with you when buying a stand, so you can check that it will fit. You can also get a dowelling jig designed for the three most common dowel sizes (6, 8 and 10mm).

Glue gun

This mains-powered tool dispenses hot-melt adhesive at the squeeze of a trigger; it is invaluable when assembling woodworking joints. The adhesive comes in sticks that you insert into the back of the gun.

Vice

You can grip large workpieces in the jaws of your portable workbench. However, for smaller items it is useful to have a bench-mounted vice. Traditional metal workshop vices are clamped in place; you can also buy a lightweight resin vice that fits into the holes in your workbench jaws.

Drill stand

Bench hook

Vice

Glue gun

Clamps

Glue sticks

Choosing screws and wall fixings

Whatever you are fixing to a wall – shelving or curtain rails, for example – it is always essential to provide good, strong fittings suitable for the load and to use appropriate screws.

Most of the fixings you make will require countersunk screws. Traditionally, all screws had slotted heads and were driven with a flat-tip screwdriver. Today, most screws are designed for driving with a power screwdriver and their heads have a specially shaped recess to engage the screwdriver tip more positively than a flat-tip driver does in a slot. The most common recesses are cross-shaped.

Phillips These screws have a simple cross and are found mainly in flat-pack furniture kits and on domestic appliances.

Pozidriv and Prodrive A star-shaped recess grips the screwdriver tip more securely than a slotted head. Drivers for Pozidriv and Prodrive screws are interchangeable. In each case the No. 2 size will drive screws up to gauge 10.

Woodscrews Traditional woodscrews are threaded only for part of their length. Many modern countersunk screws have continuously threaded shanks and other features, such as twin threads that are designed to make them quicker and easier to drive. For everyday use, store a small selection of Pozidriv or Prodrive countersunk woodscrews in individual containers. The most useful sizes are: 19, 25, 38 and 50mm in gauge No. 8; 50 and 75mm in gauge No. 10.

Other screw head types Raised countersunk and round-head woodscrews usually have slotted heads. Other head types you may encounter – especially in flat-pack furniture kits and on domestic appliances – include internal-hex screws with a plain hexagonal recess, driven with an Allen key; Torx screws and Uni-screws with specially shaped hexagonal recesses; and Robertson screws with a square recess. Each type requires a special screwdriver.

Fixings for solid walls

For masonry walls Use screws that will penetrate the wall by a minimum of 50mm, driven into plastic wall plugs that match the screw gauge.

On timber-framed walls Where the screws pass directly into the framing, 40mm penetration will be adequate unless a heavy load is to be put on the shelves, when screws should go in by 50mm. Before putting up any fixing, always use a battery-powered cable detector to locate cables or pipes buried in walls.

Masonry nail A hardened, galvanised nail that will penetrate and grip when driven into bricks or blocks. Masonry nails are not suitable for use in concrete or hard stone.

Masonry nails offer a fast way of fixing timber battens to brick walls. Choose a length that will penetrate beyond the fixing by about 15mm into bare masonry or about 25mm into a plastered wall: nails typically come in lengths from 25mm to 100mm. Hammer the nails in with short, positive strokes: they will not bend and will shatter if not struck squarely, so wear eye protection while you work.

Round-head Pozidriv

Round-head slotted

Countersunk slotted

Countersunk Pozidriv

Woodscrew and wall plug The fibre or plastic plug expands to fit the hole and grip the masonry wall. Plugs are in lengths from 15mm to 90mm.

For lightweight fittings, use No. 8 gauge screws and matched plugs. For heavier fittings use No. 10 or No. 12 gauge screws. The screw should be long enough to extend about 25mm into the masonry after passing through the fitting and the plaster.

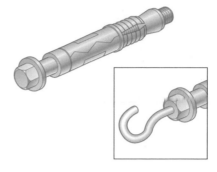

Expansion or anchor bolt This is a bolt with a segmented metal shield. The shield fits into a drilled hole in masonry and then expands to grip the hole sides when the bolt is tightened. Bolts range from about 5mm to 25mm in diameter, and come in lengths to fix objects from about 10mm to

Hammer-in fixing or nail plug A screw with a special thread for easy driving, ready-fitted into a nylon sleeve. It can be tapped with a hammer into a drilled hole. Lengths typically 50mm to 160mm will fix objects from about 5mm to 110mm thick.

A strong, fast method for fixing a lot of timber battens to brick or concrete. Also suitable for lightweight fixings into building blocks. The hole should extend 5–15mm beyond the screw tip. So for a screw 50mm long fixing a 10mm thick object, make wall holes at least 45mm deep.

Frame fixing A long screw ready-fitted into a nylon wall plug. Drill the hole through the frame into the wall, push or lightly tap the fixing through and tighten with a screwdriver. Lengths to secure frames from about 20mm to 110mm thick. A secure and convenient method of fixing new or replacement door or window frames to walls. Useful for repairing a door frame that has worked loose. As a guide, the depth of the masonry hole should be at least five times the diameter of the plug.

STANDARD WALL PLUGS

Finned plastic tapered plug with split end to allow expansion, and either fins or lugs to prevent it turning in the hole. A rim of flexible ears prevent it being pushed in too far. Each size will accept screws of several lengths and gauges.

Ribbed plastic Has no fins or lugs, but the shallow, lengthways ribs prevent it from turning in the hole. Sold in colour-coded sizes.

Strip plastic Straight-sided plug with shallow lengthways ribs. Can be bought in strips and cut to length with a trimming knife. Sold in colour-coded sizes.

Fibre Straight-sided plug of tough, compressed fibre. Sold in various lengths but can be cut with a trimming knife. Becoming obsolete but still available.

120mm thick. The bolt head may be fixed, fitted with a nut and washer or hook or eye shaped (see inset, previous page).

A very strong, heavy-duty fixing suitable for objects such as wall cupboards, garage doors, lean-to framework or fence and gateposts fixed to masonry. A fixed-head bolt (known as a loose bolt) is pushed through the fixture before being screwed into the shield. A nut-head (or projecting) bolt is placed in the hole with the shield and the fitting is hung on it before the nut and washer are fitted. The masonry hole needs to be wider than the hole through the fitting – generally 6mm wider than the bolt diameter.

Steel sleeve anchor or expansion bolt Steel bolts with an expanding wedge at the end for gripping against the sides of a drilled hole. Bolts have screw-on nuts and washers. Sizes are available for fixing objects ranging from about 5mm to 110mm thick.

Easy, quickly fitted heavy-duty fixing for things such as door and window frames, trunking or hand rails. The hole can be drilled through the frame and masonry at the same time, and is the same diameter for both the fitting and the masonry. Bolt diameters typically range from 5mm to 20mm.

Plugging compound For making fixings in holes that have become enlarged because of the drill bit wandering or because a previous fixing has failed. It is supplied in a two-colour putty-like strip. Cut off the amount required with scissors. Take off the protective film and knead the strip. When the blue pigment turns white, the compound is ready for use.

Fixings for hollow walls, ceilings and lightweight blocks

Woodscrew and plug The screw has a winged plastic plug that spreads out to grip the back of a wall or ceiling board. The plug can be re-used if the screw is withdrawn. It is designed to be used for lightweight or medium fittings to plasterboard, hardboard or plywood (including hollow doors) up to about 25mm thick. The cavity behind the board needs to be at least 15mm deep.

Machine screw and expanding rubber plug The screw fits into a nut in a rubber sleeve that is compressed to grip the back of the board. The plug stays in place if the screw is withdrawn. Plugs are sold with or without a screw. A strong fixing for plasterboard, plywood, hardboard, sheet metal, glass or plastic, up to about 45mm thick. The plug protects the screw from vibration and rusting. It can also be used as a wall plug in masonry where it shapes to the hole's contours.

Machine screw and metal cavity fixing A metal plug with a nut welded in the end. It collapses to form metal wings that grip the back of the board. A strong fixing for heavyweight fixtures to hardboard, plasterboard, chipboard, plywood and fibreboard, up to about 35mm thick.

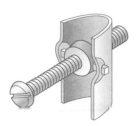

Gravity toggle A machine screw with a swinging metal bar (toggle) attached. When the screw is inserted, the toggle swings down and grips the back of the wall. It is lost if the screw is withdrawn.

A strong fixing for plasterboard or lath-and-plaster walls. The cavity has to be at least 32mm wide, or wider for larger sizes.

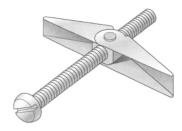

Spring toggle A machine screw fitted with a spring-operated toggle bar that folds back while it is being inserted and then springs open when it is inside the cavity. The toggle is lost if the screw is withdrawn. The typical size range is for screws 50–80mm long.

A strong fixing for plasterboard or lath-and-plaster walls and ceilings. The cavity has to be at least 45mm wide – even wider for larger sizes. The toggle can be used with a hook for hanging a light-fitting from the ceiling.

Nylon toggle and collar A nylon collar that takes a wood screw and is linked by a notched nylon strip to a toggle. After insertion, the strip is used to draw the toggle towards the collar to take the screw tip and grip the back of the board. It is then cut off. Typical size is for No. 6 woodscrews. The collar closes the drilled hole and the adjustable fitting is used for fixing to plasterboard, lath-and-plaster or suspended ceilings of different thicknesses. The toggle is retained if the screw is withdrawn.

SPECIAL TYPES OF WALL PLUG

Winged-arrow type
Light plastic plug that spreads out to grip the back of plasterboard. For use with No. 8 screws and lightweight fixings. It can be re-used.

Expanding-wing type
The wings are forced apart to grip the back of the board. Small-sized plugs are for use with No. 6 screws in hollow doors. Longer-sized plugs with No. 8 screws for medium-weight fixings to board. Cannot be re-used.

Metal self-drive
A metal device with an outside thread that is screwed into plasterboard using a No. 2 Pozidriv screwdriver. The flange on the head prevents it from pushing through the plasterboard. A nylon verson is also available for lightweight fixings.

Nylon rivet anchor
The plug is split along most its length and compressed into wings. For use with No. 8–10 screws for making fixings to plasterboard, particularly partition walls. Can be re-used.

Chipboard plug
Nylon fastener with an outside thread that is hammered into a hole drilled in chipboard. It has a split end and expands to give a secure grip. For use with No. 6, 8 and 10 screws. The plug can be re-used.

Helical wing or twist-lock type
Nylon plug with helical wings that cause it to rotate as it is tapped home and prevent it coming out if the screw is withdrawn. For use with large diameter screws to make strong fixings into aerated blocks. Can be re-used.

Choosing nails

You are likely to use oval wire nails and panel pins most frequently. Buy other types when you need them.

Oval wire nails The most commonly used nails, they have an oval cross-section and a stubby head. Position them with the oval parallel with the wood grain to avoid splitting the wood. Punch in the nail head and fill over it for an invisible fixing. Use them for securing the joints in light timber frames and other general woodwork jobs.
Sizes From 25 to 150mm; useful sizes to keep are 50 and 75mm.

Masonry nails Specially hardened round steel nails used to fix wood to masonry and preferred nowadays to cut clasp nails. They are hard to remove and can shatter while being driven.
Sizes From 25 to 100mm.

Annular (ring-shank) nails A ridged shank grips wood better than a smooth wire nail. They are used where the fixing has to resist being pulled apart and are almost impossible to remove. Particularly good for making fixings into man-made boards.
Sizes From 20 to 100mm.

Round wire nails These have a round cross-section and a large flat head. Used on rough woodwork, such as the framework for a partition wall or a garden pergola.
Sizes From 25 to 150mm.

Clout nails Short, galvanised nails with a wide flat head, used for fixing roof tiles and slates. Felt nails are shorter versions, which are designed for fixing roofing felt.
Sizes 50 and 75mm for clout nails and 12 and 25mm for felt nails.

Cut nails Traditional nails cut from flat metal sheet. Cut clasp nails are still used to fix wood to masonry (skirting boards, for example), while cut floor nails – also known as floor brads – are used to fix floorboards to their joists.
Sizes Various sizes are available.

Panel pins Have a round cross-section and a small flat head. As the name implies, they are used chiefly for fixing thin sheet materials to an underlying timber framework. They are also ideal for fixing timber mouldings in place, although pilot holes for the pins may be needed in small mouldings to avoid splitting the wood. Hardboard panel pins have a diamond-shaped head that is driven in flush with the board surface, and often have a coppered finish.
Sizes From 15 to 50mm; useful sizes to keep are 20, 25 and 40mm.

Plasterboard nails Have a cone-shaped head (like a countersunk screw) and a jagged shank to grip the framing to which the board is being fixed. They have a galvanised finish.
Sizes 30 and 40mm, for fixing 9.5 and 12.7mm thick plasterboard respectively.

Drill accessories

Apart from drilling holes, your cordless drill can do a number of other jobs if fitted with the right accessory. Here are some of the most useful.

Wire brushes
Remove rust or old paint from metal surfaces with one of these. There are two types, cups and wheels, both available in a range of sizes. Between them they will allow you to get into awkward corners as well as tackling flat surfaces. Most have a built-in spindle; some have a separate spindle called an arbor so you can fit different brushes on one spindle.

Sanding attachments
These good all-rounders allow you to carry out small-scale sanding jobs on flat surfaces if you do not have a power sander. Sanding discs fit on a stiff rubber backing disc and are held on by a washer and screw. Their only disadvantage is that they can leave swirl marks across the grain of the wood if you use too coarse a paper. Make sure you finish a job with medium or fine grades for a very smooth, unmarked surface. Paper discs are fine for sanding wood if the job is reasonably small. For bigger jobs with wood, or with metal or masonry surfaces, choose more durable abrasive-coated metal discs instead. Coarse discs can remove material very quickly. Flap-wheel sanders have tongues of double-sided abrasive paper fixed to a centre spindle and are good for sanding curved surfaces. Also useful for curves are drum sanders. They consist of a thick disc of foam plastic, coated with abrasive paper.

Polishing pads
Take the hard work out of polishing your car's paintwork or the furniture with a lambswool pad or bonnet, which fits over the rubber backing pad of a disc sander. Foam drum polishers work in a similar way.

Paint mixers
To mix and stir paint and other mixes such as wallpaper paste and tile grout, fit one of these to your drill. They are made of plastic or metal and will give paint or other liquids a thorough mixing. A powerful drill will also be able to mix plaster. Use mixers only with a slow speed setting on your drill to avoid splashing.

Light-duty pump
This accessory can cope with jobs such as emptying a garden pond or mopping up after a plumbing disaster. The drill drives an impeller inside the pump casing that has inlet and outlet spigots to take lengths of standard garden hose. Make sure you use the manufacturer's recommended setting on your drill.

Hole saws
If you have to cut a perfectly round hole in a piece of wood, the best way to do it is with a hole saw (see page 18). It is a cylinder of steel with teeth at one end and a central twist drill that makes the starting hole. Hole saws can be bought singly or in sets, and can cut holes of up to 75mm in diameter.

Polishing bonnet and backing pad

Pump

Wire brushes

Paint mixer

Sanding discs and rubber backing disc

Basic skills

Sizing up

Many DIY jobs involve three essential but unrelated jobs: measuring the size of things; positioning them to a true horizontal or vertical; and checking that making fixings will not cause damage to cables or pipework. Here are the tools you need for these jobs, and how to use them.

Measuring up

A retractable tape measure consists of a coil of printed steel stored on a spring-loaded drum within a plastic or metal case. The spring retracts the extended tape back into the case, which usually has a simple lock to hold the tape in the extended position if required. The strip has a slight curve in cross-section to keep it stiff when in use, and measurements are printed on the concave face, usually in metric and imperial. A 5m tape is long enough to take room measurements without being unnecessarily bulky to carry in the pocket.

1 To take an internal measurement (of an alcove, for example), hold the free end against one surface and extend the tape until the side of the case is against the opposite surface. Add the width of the case to the last measurement visible on the tape where it emerges from the case. The case width is usually printed on the case, but is typically 50 or 65mm. Always read off and mark measurements with the eye vertically above the tape if it is horizontal, or level with the tape if it is vertical. If you do not do this, a visual error called parallax occurs and the mark you make will be inaccurate. Always measure and mark twice to eliminate the risk of introducing this error.

2 The end of the tape is fitted with a small metal lug. To take an external measurement (of a piece of wood, for example), hook the lug over one end of the wood and draw the tape out until you can read off and mark the measurement.

Checking horizontals and verticals

A spirit level tells you whether surfaces are truly horizontal or vertical. It consists of a metal or plastic bar with parallel edges into which one or more clear plastic vials are set. The vial in the long edge of the level indicates a true horizontal, while vials at each end indicate a true vertical. Each vial contains an air bubble and is marked with two parallel lines. When the bubble is centred between the marks, the tool is level or vertical according to which vial is being used. Long spirit levels are more accurate than short ones; buy a spirit level at least 300mm long and ideally 1m long.

1 To check a horizontal, rest the level on the surface being checked and view the vial in the long edge from directly above or beside the level. Adjust the surface until the bubble is precisely centred between the marks on the vial.

2 To check a vertical, hold the level against the surface and view the vial at the end with the eye at the same level. Adjust the position of the surface until the bubble is centred in the vial.

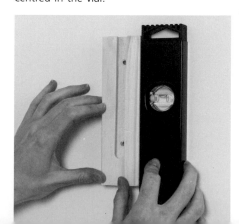

3 Some spirit levels have one end vial set in a movable mounting marked with an angle scale. Rotate the mounting to the required angle and use the level to set a surface to that specific angle. However, this is less accurate than other tools for this job, such as a sliding bevel.

Locating concealed hazards

A cable and pipe detector is a hand-held, battery-powered electronic device that will reveal the presence of electricity cables or plumbing pipework concealed in the house structure. It is important to be aware of their presence whenever you are making fixings (with nails or with screws and wallplugs) into a wall, floor or ceiling, since piercing one could cause personal injury, physical damage or both.

In some cases it is obvious where buried services are located. For example, you can expect there to be a vertical cable run immediately above a light switch or pipework above or below a flush-mounted thermostatic shower mixer valve. In other cases, using the detector can avoid a potential accident.

Some detectors will locate only live electrical cables; others will detect any buried metal – cable, pipework, even the line of nails fixing plasterboard to a hidden wall stud or ceiling joist.

Switch the detector on and set its sensitivity according to the manufacturer's instructions. Pass it slowly back and forth over the area you are testing. The detector will bleep and may flash a light when it senses a hazard, enabling you to mark and avoid its route when making any fixings.

Cutting

After measuring, your next job is to cut to size. The tools you need for this depend on what you are cutting and on how thick it is. Whichever tool you are using, make sure that it is sharp.

Using a trimming knife

A sharp trimming knife will cut all sorts of thin sheet materials, from wallpaper and soft floorcoverings to plasterboard. You can use it freehand but you will get better results if you place a steel straightedge over the cutting line and draw the knife blade along its edge. Make sure your free hand is anchoring the straightedge securely and that your fingertips are out of the way of the knife blade.

1 When using a trimming knife on the workbench or on the floor, always place a cutting board or a piece of scrap hardboard beneath whatever you are cutting. This will allow the knife to cut cleanly through the workpiece without scoring and damaging the surface below.

2 Hold the knife securely and draw it along the straightedge in one continuous movement. If necessary, make two or three passes rather than trying to cut the material in one go; the harder you have to press, the more risk there is that the blade will slip off line. Always cut against the side of the straightedge next to the waste material.

Using a hacksaw

A junior hacksaw will cut metal and rigid plastic – and wood with a small cross-section, such as timber mouldings. Make sure that the blade is fitted with the points of the teeth facing away from the handle, so it will cut on the forward stroke.

1 The hacksaw blade tends to snatch when cutting thin metal, so it is best to secure the workpiece in the jaws of your workbench. Most have grooves machined in the mating edges of the jaws for holding round objects, such as copper pipe or a metal wardrobe rail.

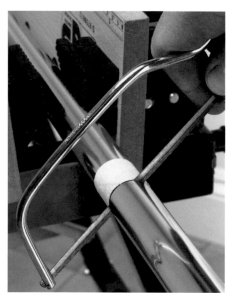

2 Start the cut on the waste side of the marked line, as for cutting wood with a tenon saw. A strip of masking tape makes a good cutting guide. Draw the blade towards you two or three times to start the cut, taking care to keep the blade on line.

3 Saw with firm forward strokes. On metal tubing, the teeth will tend to snatch as you start the cut. Do not let the blade jump out of the cut as you proceed. Complete the cut with a few gentle strokes.

Using a tenon saw

A tenon saw will cut wood and man-made boards. Its cutting depth is limited to about 75mm by the presence of the stiffening along the top edge of the blade. This also limits the width of the workpiece that can be cut; in practice, it is difficult to make a cut longer than about 300mm.

Whatever you are cutting must be held securely. You can clamp it in the jaws of your workbench, but it is easier to hold small workpieces using a bench hook (see page 19). You can buy one or make one from scrap wood and board. Glue and screw two pieces of softwood batten to opposite faces of a rectangle of plywood measuring about 250 x 150mm.

1 To cut a piece of wood to length, mark the cutting line on it. Hold it securely on your workbench with the thumb of your free hand next to the cutting line to guide the saw blade. Position the saw blade so it will cut just on the waste side of the cutting line, and draw it towards you at about 45° to start the cut.

2 Once the saw teeth begin to bite, start to cut the wood with light but firm strokes. Remember that the saw blade cuts on the forward stroke only. Start to flatten out the angle of the saw. Complete the cut with gentle strokes, holding the saw almost level with the wood surface, to avoid splitting the underside of the wood. Support the off-cut with your free hand if the workpiece is clamped in a workbench.

Fixing with screws

A screw is a stronger fixing device than a nail. Its thread grips the material into which it is driven and its head secures the item being fixed. Unlike a nail, a screw can be withdrawn easily to undo the fixing.

Different types and sizes of screws are used for different jobs (see page 20), but for everyday DIY, you will need only a small selection. You also need a screwdriver to drive screws and, to work successfully, the screwdriver tip must match the size and shape of the recess in the screw head. You can drive (and remove) screws by hand or with a cordless screwdriver or drill.

Screwing wood to wood

Start by choosing a screw with a countersunk head that is long enough to pass through the piece you are fixing and halfway into the piece you are fixing it to. The screw head will be flush with the surface once the screw has been driven in. Screws come in different diameters called gauge numbers. For most jobs you will need only two: gauge 8 screws up to 50mm long will be thick enough for most jobs; use a thicker gauge 10 screw up to 75mm long for heavier-duty fixings.

1 Mark where you want the screw hole in the piece of wood you are fixing. Fit a twist drill bit the same size as the screw shank in your drill, and drill a clearance hole right through the wood. Place scrap wood beneath the workpiece so you do not drill into your workbench.

2 Exchange the twist drill bit for a countersink bit and drill the cone-shaped recess for the screw head in the mouth of the clearance hole. It should be as wide as the screw head.

3 Hold the piece of wood you are fixing in position over the piece you are fixing it to. Push a bradawl (or a nail if you don't have one) through the clearance hole you drilled in step 1 to mark the screw position on the piece below. Drill a pilot hole 2mm in diameter at the mark to half the depth of the wood.

4 Reposition the two pieces of wood and insert the screw through the clearance hole in the top piece so it enters the pilot hole in the piece beneath. Tighten it fully with your screwdriver until the screw head is fully recessed in the countersunk hole.

Screwing into metal or plastic

You may want to make a fixing into a metal or plastic surface – for example, to mount a roller blind to a uPVC window. You need a special self-tapping screw for this sort of job. The screw needs a pilot hole and cuts its own thread as it is driven in. Self-tapping screws are made from hardened steel and come with countersunk, raised countersunk and pan heads (the last resembles a roundhead screw but with the head flattened).

Using a power screwdriver

Driving screws with a power screwdriver is much quicker and easier than driving them by hand, especially when using cross-head screws. You can use a cordless drill on a slow speed setting or buy a cordless screwdriver instead. Both tools use interchangeable screwdriver bits, which are available to fit all common screw heads. It is actually cheaper to buy a set of these bits and a cordless tool than it is to buy individual screwdrivers. You can use a power driver with slotted-head screws but there is a greater risk of the bit slipping out of the slot and damaging the workpiece than with hand screwdriving.

1 Select the screwdriver bit to match the screw size and recess type. Fit it in the drill chuck or use the magnetic bit holder supplied with the bits.

2 If you are using a cordless drill, set it to the screwdriving symbol and choose an intermediate torque setting (for example, 3 on a scale of 1 to 5).

3 Fit the screw into the tip of the screwdriver bit and offer it up to its pre-drilled hole.

4 Start the drill or screwdriver and drive in the screw. With a cordless drill, the torque setting selected should allow the clutch to slip as the screw is tightened. If this does not happen, select a different torque setting until it does.

5 Set the screwdriver or drill to reverse to undo a screw.

SCREWING INTO WALLS AND CEILINGS

You cannot simply drive a screw into most walls or ceilings to make a fixing. There are two exceptions: if you have a timber-framed partition wall and the fixing coincides with one of the vertical frame members; or, if you are making a ceiling fixing directly into a joist. In most cases, you have to drill a hole and insert a special fixing device (see pages 20–23) to hold the screw in place.

Drilling holes

There are few DIY jobs that do not involve drilling a hole at some stage. Your cordless drill is the power source for all these operations, used in conjunction with a range of drill bits and other accessories.

Fitting drill bits

Select the right type of drill bit for the job you are doing (page 15).

1 Open the chuck by twisting the knurled ring and fit the end of the drill bit inside it.

2 Tighten the locking ring until you feel it start to slip. The drill bit is now secure. Select forward gear and the drilling or hammer-drilling option, and you are ready to start work.

Drilling freehand

Most people drill holes by simply pointing the drill at the surface and squeezing the trigger. With few exceptions, drilled holes have to be at 90° to the surface.

1 If you have a good eye, check from two angles that you are holding the drill at more or less the right angle. This is good enough for many drilling jobs.

2 If you want to check the angle more accurately, hold the drill in position and set a try square against the surface you are drilling into. The drill bit should be parallel with the metal blade of the try square.

GET TO KNOW YOUR DRILL

Cordless drills run on rechargeable batteries, and all but the cheapest come with a spare to recharge while the other is in use. Check whether the battery can be left to trickle-charge for hours, or whether it has a fixed recharge time.

Make sure you are familiar with how to select the following features:
• Forward and reverse gears
• The correct speed setting for drilling and screwdriving
• Hammer action for making holes in masonry
• The correct torque setting, which enables you to apply the optimum turning force when driving screws into different materials

Drilling small holes in wood or metal

Fit a twist drill bit of the required diameter and select the drilling setting on the drill.

1 Secure the workpiece on your workbench, with some scrap wood underneath if you are drilling a hole right through it. This prevents you from damaging your bench jaws and guarantees a clean exit hole through the workpiece.

2 Hold the drill tip at the point where you need to drill and check that you are holding it upright. Drill the hole through the workpiece and on into the scrap wood. In metal, withdraw the drill bit while it is still running so that it does not jam in the hole.

Drilling large holes in wood

Fit a flat wood bit of the required size and select the drilling setting on the drill.

1 Secure the workpiece on the bench with scrap wood beneath it.

2 Position the lead point of the drill bit at the drilling mark and start drilling. As the cutting blades begin to bite and cut the hole, they will cut evenly if you are holding the drill upright. Drill on into the scrap wood, which will guarantee a clean exit hole through the workpiece.

Alternatively Clamp the wood so the drill can emerge from the underside into free air. Drill the hole until the lead point just penetrates the wood. Turn it over, relocate the lead point in the hole and drill out the rest of the hole. This will reduce the risk of leaving a rough exit hole. Use this technique for jobs such as fitting a cylinder lock to a front door.

Drill bit varieties

Apart from the basic selection of drill bits, you may need to buy others for specific DIY jobs. Long twist drills are available in lengths of up to 165mm (and 8mm in diameter). They are used for making holes in thick components such as timber-framed partition walls.

Reduced-shank drills are available in diameters up to 20mm (most standard twist drills go up to 10 or 13mm only). They have 13mm diameter shanks to fit the maximum chuck size on most cordless drills.

Nailing

A nail is one of the simplest fixing devices. Different nail types and sizes are used for different jobs, but in practice you will need only a small range to cope with everyday DIY jobs.

Using a claw hammer

A claw hammer will drive all but the smallest nails with ease, and its claw will extract nails that are misaligned or bent. Hold it near the end of the handle and watch the hammer head to make sure that it strikes the nail head squarely.

1 Hold the nail between your thumb and forefinger and start it with a few gentle taps of the hammer head. Check that it is at right angles to the surface.

2 Release the nail and drive it in with harder blows. For large nails, keep your wrist stiff and swing hammer and forearm from the elbow. On rough work, hammer the nail head in flush with the surface.

Using a pin hammer

A pin hammer or lightweight ball-pein hammer (shown here) is easier to handle when driving small panel pins, tacks, upholstery nails and glazing sprigs (used to hold glass panes in wooden window frames).

1 Hold the pin between your thumb and forefinger and tap it in with the flat end of the hammer head.

2 When it stands by itself, drive it in with the hammer head, flexing your wrist to control the hammer. Drive the pin fully home, or use a nail punch to recess its head in the wood, if necessary.

Removing a bent nail

If you bend a nail as you drive it, stop and remove it. Do not try to straighten a bent nail or drive it fully home at an angle. Pull it out and replace it with a new nail.

Place a piece of card or thin wood on the surface beside the nail. Hook the hammer claw under the nail head and pull the handle towards you to draw out the nail. Keep the handle vertical so you do not widen the opening of the nail hole.

Using a staple gun

A hand-operated staple gun fires metal staples, and can be used for many light fixing jobs. The staples work like two-pronged nails, relying on the crossbar between the pins to fix the material in place. Take care not to fire the gun unless its baseplate is securely pressed against the workpiece.

1 If the model accepts staples of different lengths, select the correct size for the job in hand. Load the magazine and test the gun by firing a staple into some scrap material.

2 Position the material to be fixed. Place the staple gun over the fixing position and squeeze the trigger to fire the staple. Repeat the process to make further fixings, reloading the magazine if it runs out.

Gripping and tightening

Around the house you will have to tackle a variety of small jobs where you need to get a grip on something.

You might need to tighten up a plumbing fitting that has started to weep a little water, or to dismantle a tap to change a tap washer. If you have taken down something fixed to a wall, you may want to remove the old wallplugs and fill the holes before fixing it somewhere else. Your tool kit should contain an assortment of gripping tools to help you to improvise solutions to problems like these.

Adjustable spanners

Spanners tighten and loosen nuts and bolts, which generally have hexagonal or square heads. There are more types of spanner than almost any other tool, but you can cover yourself for most domestic jobs with a couple of adjustable spanners. These have one fixed and one movable jaw, which you adjust with a worm-drive screw.

The largest nuts you are likely to have to tackle around the house are those on plumbing fittings and connectors, which are generally between 25 and 30mm 'across the flats' – measured from opposite sides of the nut. An adjustable spanner big enough to cope with these can also be used on smaller nuts.

1 To work on a nut, open the jaws of the spanner and slip it into place.

2 Tighten the movable jaw so the spanner grips opposite flats on the nut securely.

3 Work out which way to turn the nut. A nut is screwed on in a clockwise direction, so your spanner must move in the same direction to tighten the nut, and counter-clockwise to loosen it. Use reasonable force to turn the spanner as required.

4 Some jobs need two spanners. For example, to tighten a leaking brass compression fitting joining two lengths of copper pipe, you need one spanner to grip the hexagonal ring in the middle of the fitting, and the other to tighten the leaking nut where the pipe enters it.

Pliers

Pliers were originally designed for cutting, bending and twisting wire. However, you can use pliers for all sorts of everyday gripping jobs. Here are a few examples.

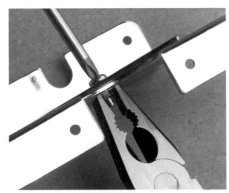

1 Use pliers to grip small nuts if you do not have a suitable spanner. For example, attaching a metal curtain track to its wall brackets may involve tightening a nut onto a small screw with a slotted head. Pliers are ideal for holding the nut while you do up the screw with a screwdriver. Pliers will also grip a ballvalve piston while you unscrew its end cap to replace a failed washer, and will turn off the lockshield valve on a radiator if you need to remove it.

2 Use pliers to remove the metal base of a broken light bulb from its lampholder. Turn off the power at the mains, then push the tip of the pliers into the base of the bulb and turn it counter-clockwise to remove.

3 Use pliers to pull unwanted wallplugs out of the wall. When you have unscrewed whatever was fixed to the wall, drive the screw back into the plug for a few turns, then grip the screw head with the pliers and pull screw and plug straight out. Fill the hole for an invisible repair.

Self-locking wrench

This tool can be used as a spanner, a wrench (for gripping round objects such as metal tubing), pliers and even as a simple clamp. The jaws can be adjusted to a range of settings and then locked into place.

1 Close the jaws onto whatever you want to grip by squeezing the handles, and turn the adjuster screw counter-clockwise until the handles close.

2 If the workpiece is too small for the tool to lock, keep squeezing the handles and turn the adjuster screw clockwise until the jaws touch the work. Operate the release lever, turn the adjuster a little more and squeeze the handles to lock the jaws.

3 To release the locking action, hold the handles together and operate the release lever.

Making wall fixings

Fixing things to walls is the key part of many everyday DIY jobs, from fitting shelves and curtain tracks to putting up a mirror or hanging a display cabinet. It is an easy job as long as you use the right fixings and the correct technique. Done wrongly, the fixing will fail with potentially serious consequences.

Assessing the job

The first step is to discover what sort of wall is involved, because this dictates how you make a fixing into it.
• Masonry walls sound solid when tapped; most exterior walls and internal ground-floor walls are of this type.
• Timber-framed internal partition walls and ceilings sound hollow when they are tapped, whether they are clad with plasterboard or the lath and plaster found in pre-1945 houses.
• Dry-lined masonry walls also sound hollow when they are tapped. This is because they have a layer of lath and plaster (you will find this in pre-1945 houses) or plasterboard on a framework of timber battens attached to the masonry, instead of solid plaster.
• Timber-framed houses have dry-lined plasterboard walls throughout.

Masonry walls

For fixings in solid masonry, you have to drill a hole in the wall and insert a hollow wallplug that will grip a screw when one is driven into it. To make a secure fixing, the plug and screw must penetrate solid masonry to a minimum depth of 25mm. On a plastered wall you must therefore make an additional allowance for the thickness of the plaster (about 13mm in a modern house and up to 20mm in older houses).

For heavy-duty fixings the screw must penetrate up to 40mm, so use a 50 or 63mm screw.

Choosing wallplugs

Moulded plastic wallplugs are available in a range of sizes in two main types: smooth and flanged. Smooth plugs fit entirely within the drilled hole, with the neck of the plug just below the wall surface. Flanged plugs have a surface flange that fits flush with the wall surface. Choose a plug to match the length and gauge of the screw you intend to use. The drill diameter to use will be marked on the plastic 'tree' to which the plugs are fixed, or on the packaging.

Frame plugs are moulded plastic or expanding metal wallplugs with an extended sleeve, and are designed for fixing timber door and window frames to walls.

Making the fixing

Fit a masonry drill bit of the required size in the drill chuck. Select the drilling setting (or hammer action if you have it) on the drill. If it has two speed settings, select the lower speed.

1 Measure the length of the wallplug you intend to use, and wrap a piece of visible tape round the drill bit to act as a depth mark. Position it at a distance of 5mm plus the plug length from the tip of the bit.

2 Press the tip of the bit against the wall where you plan to drill and check by eye that the drill is at right angles to the surface.

3 Start the drill and apply firm pressure to drill out the hole. On deep holes, withdraw the bit once or twice so the flutes on the drill bit can clear dust from the hole.

4 Drill until the tape reaches the wall surface, then withdraw the bit while the drill is still running to clear drill dust from the hole.

5 Insert the wallplug to check that it will fit. Pass the screw through whatever you are fixing and drive it into the wallplug. If the plug turns in the hole as you tighten the screw you have made the hole too large and the fixing will fail. Pull the plug out and fit a larger one.

Using frame plugs

These plugs come in a range of sizes to suit different frame thicknesses. They are sold complete with long wood screws or special hammer-in screws.

1 Set the frame in position and mark the locations of the fixings. If possible, ensure that they will be made into solid masonry, not into the mortar joints between courses.

2 Choose a twist drill bit to match the diameter of the frame plug. Select drilling and high speed on your drill. Drill a clearance hole through the frame at each fixing location. Stop drilling and withdraw the still-rotating drill bit to clear the debris.

3 Switch to a masonry drill bit of the same diameter. Select hammer action (if you have it) and low speed on your drill. Measure the length of the frame plug and wrap a piece of tape round the drill bit to act as a depth mark. Position it at a distance of 5mm plus the plug length from the tip of the bit.

4 Insert the drill bit through the clearance hole until it touches the masonry, and start drilling the hole there. Withdraw the drill bit at intervals to clear the debris. Drill until the tape depth stop reaches the surface of the frame.

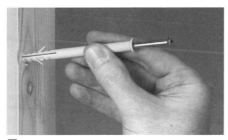

5 Insert the frame plug and tap it fully home with a hammer so its flange is flush with the frame. Drive in the wood screw or the hammer-in screw to complete the fixing.

Partition walls and ceilings

You can make fixings into internal partition walls and ceilings in one of two ways.
• Locate the wall frame members (the studs) or the ceiling joists, and screw through the cladding into solid timber. To do this, you need to use an electronic joist detector (see page 29), or make some test drillings through the cladding. In modern houses, wall studs and ceiling joists are at 400mm centres. In older houses the spacings may be as wide as 450mm or even 600mm.
• If the stud or joist positions do not coincide with where you want to make your fixings, drill a hole in the cladding and insert a cavity fixing device that will expand and grip the inner face of the cladding. The device must be strong enough to support the load on the fixing.

Choosing cavity fixings

A wide range of cavity fixings is available, made from moulded plastic or metal. The fixing is inserted through a hole in the wall cladding, and a wood screw (or the

machine screw supplied with the fixing) is tightened into it. This draws up and compresses part of the fixing against the inner face of the wall cladding, providing a firm grip for the screw. The fixing remains in place in the wall if the screw is removed.

Spring toggles (page 40) have two spring-loaded wings that flip outwards once the fixing is inserted, to grip the inner face of the wall cladding. The toggle is lost in the cavity if the screw is removed.

Cavity fixings are sold as suitable for light, medium or heavy loads. As a general rule, use plastic or metal screw-in fixings (above) for light loads. Use plastic anchor fixings or spring toggles for medium loads, and metal anchor fixings for heavy loads such as a wall cabinet or radiator. The metal anchor fixing has four wings that grip against the inner face of the wall cladding as the machine screw is tightened.

Making the fixing

You can drill through plasterboard or lath-and-plaster with a twist drill bit. Match the drill size to the fixing you are using. Select the drilling setting on your drill, and high speed on a two-speed drill.

1 Press the tip of the drill bit into the surface and check by eye that the drill is at right angles to the surface. Drill until the drill bit breaks through the cladding, and withdraw it while it is still rotating to clear debris from the hole.

2 Push the fixing into the hole until its flange is flush with the surface. Remove the machine screw if one is supplied (except for spring toggles).

3 Pass the machine screw (or wood screw) through whatever you are fitting. Drive the screw into the fixing and tighten it fully.

Spring toggles

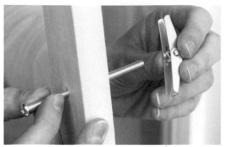

1 Do not put a spring toggle straight into its hole. Instead, remove the machine screw and pass this through whatever you are fitting.

2 Reattach the toggle to the screw, fold up its wings and push them through the hole. Check that the wings have opened by pulling on the fixing, then tighten the screw fully.

Dry-lined walls

Dry-lined walls have a cavity 25–40mm wide between the lining and the solid masonry behind it. How you make a fixing depends on the load to be supported. For lightweight items, you can use plastic or metal screw-in fixings as for partition walls. Medium-weight items need a cavity anchor but the cavity depth restricts the types of fixing you can use. Heavyweight items must be supported on fixings made into the masonry using a long screw and wallplug. The best type is a frame plug long enough to pass through wall cladding and cavity, and penetrate masonry by about 40mm.

Making the fixing

Use a twist drill to match the diameter of the frame plug to make a hole in the wall cladding at the fixing location, then switch to a long masonry drill bit of the same size. Wrap tape round it to indicate the total drilling depth (cladding plus cavity plus 40mm). Select drilling (or hammer action if your drill has it) and slow speed.

1 Insert the masonry drill bit through the hole in the wall cladding and check that it is at right angles to the surface.

2 Drill the hole to the depth indicated by your tape depth stop. Withdraw the drill bit from time to time to clear the hole of debris, which will fall into the cavity.

3 Insert the frame plug and check that its flange fits flush with the surface of the wall cladding. Pass the screw through whatever you are fixing and drive it into the plug.

Timber-framed houses

In a timber-framed house, internal walls are timber-framed partitions and you should make fixings into them as described on page 39. External walls are lined with plasterboard but behind this is a vapour barrier and a layer of glass-fibre insulation. Fixings should be made into the vertical timber frame members wherever possible. Otherwise use cavity fixings, as for other partition walls.

Fixings in external walls

Use a twist drill bit to match the size of the fitting. Select drilling and high speed on the drill. Press the tip of the drill bit into the wall surface and check by eye that the drill is at right angles to the surface.

Drill until the drill bit just breaks through the wall cladding. If you drill any deeper, you will penetrate the vapour barrier and the drill bit will pull tufts of insulation out of the hole. Insert the cavity fixing and screw whatever you are fitting into place.

Making good

Making good means restoring something to its original state. Woodwork can be dented or split. Plaster can crack or come away from the surface beneath. Gaps can appear where skirting boards and architraves meet the wall. All these defects need making good, using the appropriate filler or sealant and the right tools.

Choosing fillers

There is a daunting array of fillers available in DIY stores, ranging from traditional dry powder that you mix with water to ready-mixed products in tubes, tubs, tins and cartridges. Powder fillers can be kept for a long time if they are stored in dry conditions, whereas ready-mixed fillers have a finite shelf life. Buy them only if you have a lot of filling to do in a short space of time and are likely to use up most of the filler.

You need three basic types of filler for everyday DIY: a filler for wood; a filler for plaster; and a filler for gaps. So-called 'all-purpose' fillers are available but, as with all products of this type, their performance is a compromise. They will fill anything

adequately but you will get better results with a one-job filler designed specifically for its purpose.

Repairing woodwork

Existing woodwork, whether painted or varnished, can become dented or chipped from everyday wear and tear. These defects need filling before the surface is given a new finish. Use interior wood filler on woodwork that will be painted, and wood stopper in a matching wood shade for woodwork that will be varnished.

There are also two-part products for really tough filling jobs. They consist of a basic filler and a chemical hardening agent. To start the setting process, you add a small amount of the hardening agent to activate the ingredients of the filler. This type of filler is particularly good for repairing damage caused by rot.

1 Sand the damaged area with fine wet-and-dry abrasive paper. This will smooth any rough edges to the damage and will key the surface so that the filler will bond better to it. Wipe away any dust with kitchen roll moistened with white spirit.

2 Use your filling knife to press wood filler or stopper into the damage, leaving it a little proud of the surrounding surface. Leave it to set hard.

3 Sand the filled area smooth with fine abrasive paper, then wipe away dust with kitchen roll as in step 1. The repair is now ready for redecorating.

FILLERS FOR WOODWORK

Most of the woodwork round the house will be painted or varnished and, unless it is brand new, will need to have dents and scratches filled before being finished.
• If the wood is to be painted over, standard wood filler in a tub will be adequate. Some are white and others come in a neutral, woody colour.
• If you are filling wood that is stained or varnished, you need a matching filler – called wood stopping. It comes in a range of colours and you can mix in a little woodstain to get a perfect match.
• A specialist filler is linseed oil putty – used for fixing glass into wooden window frames. Soft enough to allow the glass to be bedded into it, it sets rock hard and can be painted after a fortnight.

Repairing plaster

1 To fill a hole or crack in plaster, rake out loose material with the blade of your filling knife, leaving only the sound plaster.

2 Use an old paintbrush to brush out any dust remaining in the hole. It is important to make the area as clean as possible.

3 Load some filler onto your knife and draw the blade firmly across the hole or crack to press the filler into it. Repeat as necessary to fill the entire length of a crack, then draw the blade along it to smooth off any excess filler.

PROBLEMS WITH PLASTER

Plaster is a hard but brittle material, so it may develop cracks or dents if it is knocked. It will also crack if the structure to which it is stuck moves, as often happens with the plaster on timber-framed walls and ceilings.

Use a ready-mixed wall filler for repairing small cracks and dents, and ready-mixed plaster for patching larger areas. To fill gaps where a hard-setting filler keeps falling out, use a non-setting mastic sealant instead (see Filling gaps, below).

4 Allow the filler to set hard, then sand by hand or with a power sander, using fine abrasive paper. Dust off any fine particles. The surface is now ready for redecoration.

Filling gaps

Houses are full of problem gaps – where walls meet ceilings, along the join between skirting boards or architraves and walls, around window frames and along the back edges of kitchen worktops. These are difficult to fill with conventional hard-setting fillers because the gap expands or contracts as temperature and humidity changes, and this cracks the filler.

A non-setting mastic bonds to both surfaces and stretches to accommodate the movement. Different types are available for different jobs, but an acrylic decorator's mastic or sealant is ideal for most interior filling jobs in areas that will remain dry. Apply it with a cartridge gun. It comes in white only but can be painted over.

For areas that get damp, such as a bathroom or kitchen, use a waterproof silicone sealant. It is white, and can be painted over if desired.

1 Once you have chosen which sealant or mastic is suitable for the job, cut the nozzle of the cartridge at an angle so it will extrude a bead of mastic a little wider than the gap you need to fill.

2 Most cartridges are made to fit a standard gun, so once you have the gun, all you need each time is the appropriate cartridge. Insert the cartridge in the gun and pump the trigger until the plunger touches the base of the cartridge.

3 Gently squeeze the trigger. This will push the plunger down through the cartridge and begin to force mastic out of the nozzle.

4 Hold the nozzle at 45° to the crack and draw the nozzle along it, squeezing the trigger to maintain a steady flow of mastic. The flow rate should match the speed of the nozzle as you move it along the gap. Do not leave any gaps. If you do, go back and fill them afterwards.

5 When you have filled the gap, press the piston release lever on the gun to stop the flow of mastic. Smooth the surface of the mastic with a clean, wetted fingertip. When the mastic has hardened sufficiently, you can paint over it.

Using a jigsaw

A jigsaw with a 400-500 watt motor is adequate for most DIY tasks, though you may want extra power when you discover how useful this tool is.

A jigsaw will cut wood, man-made boards and several other materials if it is fitted with the correct type of blade. You can buy a basic model very cheaply. Key features to look out for are variable speed, an adjustable soleplate so you can make cuts at angles other than 90°, and some means of collecting or extracting sawdust – either a dust bag or an adaptor so you can connect it to a vacuum cleaner. Some jigsaws now feature blade clamps that do not need tools. If the saw is not sold with a carry and storage case, you can buy one from DIY stores to keep the tool safe when you are not using it.

Making a short cut

Select the right blade for the job and fit it in the blade clamp. Secure whatever you are sawing to the workbench with a clamp or by holding it in the bench jaws. The saw will tend to snatch at the workpiece if you simply hold it with your free hand.

1 You can make short cuts freehand – for example, to cut a wall batten or a piece of skirting board to length. Mark the cutting line and rest the front of the saw's soleplate on the edge of the workpiece.

2 Start the saw at a slow speed and move it forwards so that the blade starts to cut just on the waste side of the cutting line. Make sure the soleplate is flat on the surface of the workpiece.

3 As the cut proceeds, increase the saw speed and check that you are keeping the blade on line. As you complete the cut, support the off-cut with your free hand. Stop the saw as soon as the blade is free.

SAFETY TIP

Many DIY tools need sharp blades or powerful motors to be able to do their jobs properly. This means that they can cause injury if they are not used correctly and with care. Never bypass or deactivate any safety guard fitted to the tool.

CHOOSING JIGSAW BLADES

Blades for cutting wood and man-made boards come in fine, medium and coarse versions; the closer the teeth, the finer the cut. The maximum cutting depth is usually between 50 and 75mm, depending on the blade. Wood-cutting blades will also cut plastic sheet materials. You need extra-fine blades for cutting metal, and there are also special blades available for cutting ceramic tiles and glass-reinforced plastics (GRP). Check that any blades you buy are compatible with your make of saw; not all are interchangeable between brands.

Making a long straight cut

Because the saw blade is narrow, it can wander off-line on long, straight cuts made freehand. On thick materials, there is also a tendency for the blade to deform under load, giving a cut that is not at 90° to the surface of the workpiece. To prevent the first problem, use a saw guide. To counteract the second, let the saw cut at its own speed rather than forcing it.

1 If the jigsaw is supplied with a side fence – a tee-shaped bar projecting from the side of the soleplate – you can use it to make cuts up to about 150mm from the edge of the workpiece. Clamp the fence in the required position and make a test cut on some scrap wood to check the setting.

2 Position the saw so the blade is aligned with the cutting line and the fence lies against the edge of the wood.

3 Move the saw forwards as the cut proceeds, keeping the fence against the edge of the workpiece. Allow the blade to run out of the cut at the far end.

Using a guide batten

To make a cut further from the edge of the workpiece than the fence will allow, use a guide batten. This is a strip of wood clamped across the workpiece to guide the edge of the saw's soleplate along the cut.

1 Mark the cutting line, align the saw blade with it and place the batten next to the side of the soleplate.

2 When you are happy with its position, clamp it to the workpiece and check that the clamps will not interfere with the travel of the saw. Make the cut by running the edge of the soleplate against the batten.

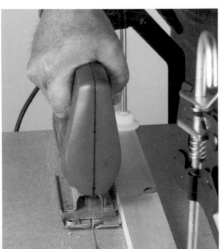

Making a curved cut

Mark the cutting line on the workpiece. Avoid starting a curved cut at the edge; the blade will skate off it as you try to start the cut. Instead, drill a hole in the waste area large enough to admit the saw blade and begin the cut there. If a curve is a continuation of a straight line, no starter hole is required.

1 Start the cut as for a straight cut, positioning the blade on the waste side of the cutting line. Move the saw forward at its own speed – don't attempt to push it – following the cutting line by eye.

2 Cut more slowly on sharp curves, turning the saw body gradually so the blade can follow it closely.

Making an internal cut-out

If you are cutting an opening in the centre of a piece of wood, you need to create a starting hole for the jigsaw blade by drilling. Mark the cut-out on the workpiece; if you are cutting a square or a rectangle, draw a line in from each corner at 45° to help you to position the drill bit. Drill a hole at each corner to give you room to turn the jigsaw blade for the next side of the cut.

1 If you use a 16mm spade bit, place the point of the bit at least 8mm into the waste area from the corner, on the 45° line. This will ensure that the drill hole does not break out of the finished cut-out shape. Drill all four holes.

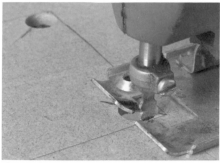

2 Insert the saw blade and rest the soleplate on the workpiece. Follow the cutting line to the next drill hole for straight cuts, or carry on cutting round a curve.

3 At the next corner, let the saw blade run right into the angle. Then turn the blade in the drill hole and start the next straight cut. Repeat at the third corner to run the saw back to your starting point.

4 Use abrasive paper to smooth the edges of the cut and to square up the internal corners.

CHOOSING ABRASIVES

Sanding discs use aluminium oxide grit as the abrasive, bonded to a strong backing fabric. If the sander has a through-the-pad dust extraction system, the sheets have holes in them that coincide with holes in the baseplate, allowing the machine to draw dust up through the pad as you work. Make sure that the discs you buy are compatible with your sander.

There is a range of disc grades, from coarse for fast removal of material to extra fine for finishing work. Some brands use a numbering system to indicate the coarseness; the lower the number, the coarser the grit. For example, 180 (coarse), 240 (medium) and 400 (fine).

Using a power sander

A random-orbit sander will cope with most everyday sanding jobs. You can buy a basic tool quite cheaply.

A random-orbit sander is the simplest of all power tools to use. Its action is designed to leave no scratch marks on the surface of wood when used with a fine grade abrasive disc. Most sanders now use touch-and-close (Velcro) fastenings to attach the abrasive discs to the sanding pad. However, these are comparatively expensive.

1 Select the correct grade of abrasive disc for the finish you want to achieve, and attach it to the sanding pad so the holes in disc and pad are aligned. Press the disc firmly into place on the pad.

2 Fit the dust bag or connect the sander to the hose of your vacuum cleaner using the adaptor provided and switch the vacuum cleaner on.

3 Hold the disc against the surface you want to sand and switch it on. Keep the sander moving backwards and forwards over the surface. You may need to start with a coarse disc to remove an old surface finish, followed by medium and then fine discs to create a smooth surface.

Choosing and buying wood

The basic raw materials for most DIY woodworking projects are softwood – cut from coniferous trees such as pine and spruce – and man-made boards. Hardwood from deciduous trees such as oak, beech, teak and mahogany is expensive and harder to work than softwood, and is used mainly for making furniture. However, hardwood mouldings are widely available and are popular because they hold detail better than the softwood equivalent.

Softwood

Softwood is not only easy to work but it almost invariably comes from renewable sources, so is not depleting valuable stocks of rare woods or destroying forests.

Buying softwood

You can buy softwood from DIY stores or from local timber merchants. Wood from timber merchants is generally cheaper and they are much more welcoming to the do-it-yourselfer than they used to be. They also stock a wider range of wood types and sizes.

However, for small amounts of wood, the convenience of the DIY store probably outweighs the extra cost involved.

Softwood sizes

Softwood is available in sawn and planed finishes, in a range of cross-sections that are described in millimetres but are still commonly referred to by their imperial equivalents – 2 x 1in equals 50 x 25mm, for example. It is important to realise that the quoted sizes are the actual dimensions of the wood when it leaves the sawmill. A piece of sawn wood described as 100 x 50mm will be that size, give or take a millimetre or so to allow for shrinkage. Planing the rough-sawn wood removes from 3mm to 6mm from each dimension, so a piece of planed wood described as 100 x 50mm (its nominal size) will actually measure about 95 x 47mm in cross-section.

To avoid mistakes when you are building things in wood, get into the habit of using the measured size of the wood you are using, rather than the nominal size, when working out dimensions.

Commonly available widths for softwood are 25, 38, 50, 75, 100, 150 and 225mm (the last usually available only in Parana pine). Common thicknesses are 12, 19, 25, 38 and 50mm.

Softwood is sold in lengths that are multiples of 300mm (known as a metric foot, and about 5mm shorter than the old imperial one). Commonly available lengths are 1.8, 2.4 and 3m.

Structural timbers, such as floor joists, are available in longer lengths.

Softwood faults

When buying softwood, check it for faults. The most serious is warping, where the wood is bent or twisted along its length.

This can be disguised when wood is sold in bundles, as in many DIY stores. Do not be afraid to open bundles and examine individual lengths before you buy, because warped wood is useless for most projects. Try to hold the timber at eye level and look along its length to check for warping. It helps to have someone with you to hold the other end.

Other faults that can spoil softwood are excessive knots – especially dead ones where the heart of the knot has fallen out – and end splits (called shakes).

Reject any wood with these faults because you will find you cannot use it when you get it home.

Hardwood

Hardwood is used in the home mainly in the form of decorative mouldings and as veneers on man-made boards. If you want a particular hardwood as an alternative to softwood – for shelves or a windowsill, for example – look for a specialist timber merchant in your local *Yellow Pages*.

Man-made boards

Man-made boards allow you to use wood wider than that available from any tree. There are two main types: boards made from real wood, glued together in thin veneers or solid strips; and, boards made from ground-up wood chips or fibres bonded together into a uniform sheet. Each has its uses, advantages and disadvantages.

Buying man-made boards

Boards of all types are available from DIY stores and timber merchants. As with

softwood, timber merchants are generally cheaper and stock a wider range of types and board sizes.

The standard board size for all types is 2440 x 1220mm, a straightforward conversion from the old imperial 8 x 4ft sheet. Most board types are also available in smaller sizes, equal to one half or one quarter of a full-sized sheet (nominally 2440 x 610mm and 1220 x 610mm), and also in 1830 x 610mm panels.

So-called furniture panels – mainly plastic-faced or veneered chipboard (see opposite) intended for shelving and making kitchen cabinets – are now made in metric sizes that are fractionally smaller than their imperial-based equivalents.

Real wood boards

The oldest of the man-made boards is plywood. Blockboard is little used today, its place in the woodworker's stockroom has been taken by timberboard (also known as stripwood).

Plywood Sheets that consist of a number of thin wood veneers called plies, bonded together with adhesive. The grain direction in each layer is at right angles to that of its neighbours, resulting in a board that is stable and equally strong in either direction. The grain direction of the outer plies (there is always an odd number) runs the length of the board.

The board surface is smooth but the edges tend to splinter when cut and can be difficult to finish neatly.

Exterior-grade (WBP) plywood is made with waterproof adhesives and is used in damp situations indoors (such as under ceramic floor tiles) as well as for outdoor structures.

Plywood with decorative hardwood outer veneers is used for making furniture and cladding flush doors.

Blockboard A board with a core of softwood strips bonded together edge to edge, and finished with one or two veneer plies on each face.

Blockboard is stronger along the length of the board than across it. It is used mainly for making decorative veneered door blanks, and is hard to find in board form. It is very expensive.

Timberboard This is a composite board that is made by gluing together parallel softwood strips to form wide boards. It is suitable for shelving, table tops and worktops and is used as an alternative to blockboard.

The boards are usually 18mm thick, and are intended for staining and varnishing.

Medium-density fibreboard (MDF) Made from fine wood fibres bonded together with resin under high pressure to create a board with a fine, even texture and smooth faces and edges. MDF is easier to cut and shape than other board types, and is now widely used for all indoor panel work as well as a wide range of flat-pack furniture.

It is available in 6, 9, 12 and 18mm thicknesses. Cutting, drilling and sanding the board produces a fine dust that can be unpleasant to inhale, so it is advisable to wear a face mask when working with it.

Fibreboard and particle board

Hardboard and chipboard were once the most widely used board types, but medium-density fibreboard (known to everyone as MDF) has now taken its place for many DIY projects.

Hardboard Made from heavily-compressed wood fibres, with one smooth surface and one with a mesh texture. It is widely available but it only comes in one thickness: 3mm.

Hardboard has little strength and is mainly used to form the back panels of cabinets and bookcases and the bases of drawers (especially in its white plastic-faced form). It is also used for jobs such as boxing-in pipes or lining timber floors where the strength of the board is unimportant. It is possible to get perforated hardboard, which is useful in workshops where tools are to be kept on the wall. Hooks fitted into the holes at the appropriate spots can make a place for every tool.

Also available is oil-tempered hardboard, which is stronger and denser than standard hardboard and can be used for outdoor projects.

Chipboard Also known as particle board. Chipboard consists of wood chips bonded together with resins. It has relatively smooth surfaces but rough, crumbly edges that can make it difficult to produce a neat finish.

Chipboard is commonly available in 12 and 18mm thicknesses. It is a heavy and dense board that blunts tools quickly, because of its high resin content. It is not as strong as plywood and has poor load-bearing strength – chipboard shelves always tend to sag unless they are well supported – and is mainly used in its plastic-faced form for kitchen units and flat-pack furniture, and in plain 22mm thick sheets for flooring. Extra-thick 28 and 38mm chipboard forms the core of laminated kitchen worktops.

Wood mouldings

Most of the wood used in woodworking is square or rectangular in cross section. Mouldings are made by machining wood to create a variety of other cross sections.

Many of these are used for structural jobs as diverse as making windows and doors and forming skirting boards and wall cladding. Other mouldings are purely decorative, being used to edge boards, to cover gaps or to trim and finish things such as built-in furniture.

Structural mouldings are generally relatively large in section and machined from softwood, although hardwood versions are available at a price. They include skirting boards, architraves, dado and picture rails, staircase handrails and balusters, windowsills and wall cladding. You can also buy structural mouldings machined from MDF and factory-primed ready for painting. They have well-finished edges and are free from knots, warping and other defects.

Decorative mouldings are machined from hardwoods such as ramin, and include small trim mouldings in quadrant, scotia, half-round and corner profiles.

Embossed trim mouldings are created by impressing decorative designs onto the face of pre-machined mouldings.

Measuring and marking wood

Accurate marking up is crucial; making a mistake at the start can spoil an entire job. Always follow the adage: measure twice, cut once.

Starting square

You can generally assume that man-made boards have edges that are square to each other. The same applies to the ends of sawn and planed softwood. However, wood or board offcuts in your workshop may not have square ends or edges, and it is very important to square them up before using them.

1 To check whether an end or edge is square, hold the stock of your try square against the adjacent edge and align the blade with the edge you are checking.

2 If it is not square, move the try square away from the corner by about 5mm and mark a line across the workpiece against the try-square blade with a trimming knife or a sharp pencil.

3 On softwood, use the try square and marker to continue the squared line onto the other faces of the workpiece. The line on the fourth face should meet up with the one on the first face.

4 Cut off the waste to leave a perfectly square end or edge.

Measuring

Use a steel ruler for measurements of less than 300mm and a tape for longer measurements. Always work in millimetres, even if you prefer to think in imperial sizes; it is easy to get confused with fractions of an inch but an exact measurement in millimetres is extremely accurate.

1 Align the end of the ruler with the squared-up end of the workpiece or hook the end of the tape over the end and extend it as required. Make sure that your eye is vertically above the figure on the ruler or tape that you want to use, and mark the workpiece at that point with a knife or pencil.

2 Hold the try square with its blade aligned with the mark, and square the cutting line across the face of the workpiece. On softwood, continue the line round the workpiece as in step 3, left.

Multiple components

Every saw cut you make removes a small amount of wood, equal to the width of the saw teeth. If you want four pieces of wood each 300mm long and you mark up four successive cutting lines 300mm apart on a length of softwood, each piece will be marginally shorter than 300mm when you cut it off. To avoid this, always mark and cut each component before marking and cutting the next.

You must also allow for the width of the saw cut when marking out man-made boards ready for cutting into a number of smaller panels. Mark parallel guide lines 3mm apart at each cutting point, instead of a single line, so you can saw between the lines when you cut the panels.

Using a combination square

You can use a combination square in the same way as a try square to mark lines at 90° to the edge of the workpiece. The design of the square also allows you to mark cutting lines at 45°.

1 Make a mark on the edge of the workpiece where you want the cutting line to begin.

2 Slide the stock to the end of the blade and hold the 45° face against the edge of the workpiece in line with the mark and with the blade extending across its width.

3 Mark the cutting line across the workpiece with a knife or sharp pencil. Alternatively, use the removable scribing pin fitted into the tool's stock.

Using a sliding bevel

A sliding bevel allows you to copy an existing cutting angle – on a replacement staircase baluster, for example – or to set a new angle using a protractor.

1 To copy an existing angle, loosen the wing nut on the tool. Hold the stock against one surface forming the angle and move the blade to touch the other surface. Tighten the wing nut to lock the blade in place.

2 To set a new angle, use a protractor to position the blade at the required angle and lock it in place.

3 Transfer the tool to the workpiece and use it like a try square to transfer the angle of the cutting line to the new wood.

Cutting wood and boards

You can use a hand or power saw for this job. Power saws save time and effort, especially for larger jobs. Whichever you use, it is important that the workpiece is held securely.

Using a bench hook

The best way of holding mouldings and other small workpieces – up to about 50 x 25mm in size – is to use a bench hook. You can buy one or make one from a piece of timber and two offcuts.

1 Place the lower batten against the near edge of your workbench and place the workpiece against the upper batten. If the batten is inset from the edge of the base, position the cutting line just beyond the end of the batten. If it is not, let the workpiece project beyond the edge of the base by about 25mm.

2 Position the saw blade just on the waste side of the cutting line, guiding it against the side of the thumb of your spare hand. Start the cut with a few light backward strokes of the saw.

3 Saw with the blade at 45° to begin with, then lower it to the horizontal once the cut is established. If the bench hook batten is inset, complete the cut by sawing into the base of the bench hook. This ensures a clean cut with no splinters on the underside. If the batten is not inset, complete the cut with gentle strokes to minimise splitting on the underside.

WORKING WITH WOOD

Using a mitre box

You can hold and cut small workpieces in a mitre box, which is itself clamped in the jaws of your workbench. The guide slots in the box allow you to make cuts at 45° as well as at 90°.

1 Mark the cutting line on the workpiece. Place it in the box with the cutting line aligned with the slots you want to use. If these do not extend to the base of the box, place a piece of scrap wood beneath the workpiece so that you can saw into it to avoid leaving a ragged finish.

2 Fit the tenon saw into the slots in the mitre box and use your free hand to hold the workpiece in place. Make the cut with the saw held horizontally. Take care not to widen the slots by letting the saw wander off line.

Using a vice

If you have a woodworking vice, you can use it to hold small workpieces while you cut them. Stick slim packing pieces of scrap wood to the vice jaws with epoxy adhesive to protect the workpiece from being marked by the steel jaws. Never tighten the jaws more than necessary to hold the piece firmly. Soft wood is easily dented.

Using a panel saw

A panel saw is used to cut wood that is too thick for the tenon saw and to cut man-made boards into smaller panels. It can be used for both cross-cutting (cutting across the grain) and ripping (cutting with the grain). Wood should not be allowed to vibrate while it is being cut, so securing it

firmly is essential to a good, clean cut and a satisfactory result.

Even when you take the greatest amount of care, it is possible that the exit cut may be a little rough. To avoid this, always start with the good side of the wood facing upwards in the bench – this way, any minor defects in the cut won't affect the finished job quite as much.

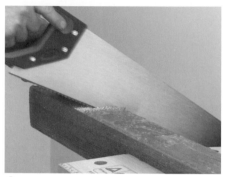

1 To cut wood across the grain, clamp it in the jaws of your workbench with the cutting line clear of the bench frame. Start the cut with a few gentle backwards strokes of the saw blade, then continue cutting with the blade at an angle of about 45°. Hold the offcut with your free hand as you complete the cut to prevent the wood from splintering on the underside.

2 To cut smaller panels from a larger sheet of board, you need to support it on both sides of the cut unless you are sawing close to the edge. Rest the panel over the open jaws of your portable workbench and saw between them, taking care not to hit the bench framework. Alternatively, rest the board on two planks supported at each end, or use an open stepladder laid on its side as a makeshift support (below).

3 Kneel over the workpiece so that your eye is above the cutting line and your arm in line with it. Start the cut on the waste side of the marked line and saw as far as is comfortable. Reposition yourself and the board to continue the cut, and complete it using short saw strokes to avoid splintering.

Using a coping saw

If the saw is already fitted with a blade, check the blade tension by tightening the screw-up handle on the tool. To fit a new blade, unscrew the handle fully and unhook the ends of the old blade from their holders. Hook the ends of the new blade into the holders, with the teeth facing away from the handle, and tighten it fully.

1 To make a cut starting at the edge of the workpiece, check that the pins on the blade holders are aligned with the frame. Start the cut with the blade at right angles to the edge. Follow the marked cutting line carefully.

2 As you saw along the cutting line, you may need to rotate the blade to stop the frame from fouling the edge of the workpiece. Unscrew the handle slightly, rotate both blade holder pins to the required angle and re-tighten the handle. Repeat as necessary to allow the blade to follow the curve.

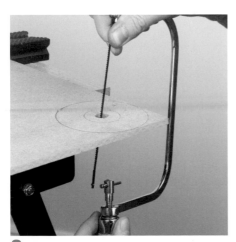

3 To make an internal cut-out, mark its outline and drill a hole through the workpiece within the waste area large enough to admit the saw blade. Unhook the blade from the frame, thread it through the hole and re-attach it to the frame.

4 Cut from the hole towards the marked outline, then follow it round until you return to your starting point. To allow the blade to turn corners in straight-sided cut-outs, drill a hole within the outline at each corner. Square up the corners with abrasive paper when you have removed the cut-out.

Using a padsaw

The padsaw is ideal for making cut-outs and cutting curves where it is not possible or practicable to use a coping saw. Two typical jobs for it are making cut-outs in plasterboard walls to fit electrical wiring accessories, and cutting keyholes in doors.

Cutting a hole in a wall

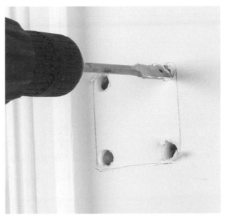

1 To make an enclosed cut, mark its outline and drill a starter hole within the waste area big enough to admit the saw blade. If the cut-out is to be square or rectangular, drill a hole at each corner so that you can turn the blade to cut along the next side.

2 Insert the saw blade and start cutting along the marked line. Use short saw strokes in a plasterboard wall to avoid damaging the cladding on the opposite side of the frame.

Cutting a keyhole

To cut a keyhole, drill the starter hole at the top and mark the sides of the slot needed to admit the tongue of the key. Insert the saw blade right through the hole and cut down both sides of the slot. Use a narrow chisel to chop out the waste wood, working from both sides of the door.

Using a hole saw

The hole saw will cut perfectly round holes in wood, man-made boards, plasterboard and sheet metal or plastic. Select the blade diameter that matches the hole you want to make and clip it into the circular arbor, or blade holder. Fit the arbor into the chuck of your power drill.

1 Locate the pilot drill bit at the centre of the cut-out and start the drill slowly. As the drill penetrates the surface, the saw teeth will start to cut into it. The cut will be even all round if you are holding the drill at a 90° angle to the surface.

2 If you are cutting a workpiece on your bench, clamp some scrap wood beneath it and saw through the workpiece into the scrap to ensure a clean exit hole.

Using a circular saw

Before you use a circular saw for the first time, read the instructions supplied with it and familiarise yourself with all the controls and safety features. Check that you have the right type of blade for the material you want to cut.

1 To remove or change a blade, make sure that the saw is unplugged. Use the Allen key provided with the saw to loosen the retaining nut. For blades with large teeth, jam a screwdriver blade between the saw teeth and the soleplate to stop it turning. For fine blades, hold the saw blade down firmly on some scrap wood. Release the old blade from its spindle, fit the replacement with the teeth pointing forwards and tighten the nut fully.

2 To set the cutting depth, place the saw on its side and loosen the lever that locks the saw body to the soleplate. Move the saw body until the saw teeth just project beyond the thickness of the material you are cutting. Tighten the lever again.

3 To make a cut up to about 150mm from the edge of the workpiece, fit the adjustable side fence in its clamp. Set it the required distance from the saw blade and tighten the wing nut. Clamp the workpiece to your workbench.

4 Rest the front edge of the soleplate on the edge of the workpiece and align the narrow guide notch with the marked cutting line. Hold the fence against the side edge of the workpiece.

5 Start the saw and let it run up to full speed, then move it forward until the blade begins to cut. Move the saw forward slowly, with its soleplate flat on the workpiece and the fence running against its side edge.

6 Let the saw run out at the end of the cut before releasing the trigger. Make sure that the blade has stopped before setting the saw down.

7 To make a cut beyond the reach of the fence, clamp a guide batten across the workpiece, parallel with the marked cutting line, and run the edge of the soleplate against it. Align the guide notch with the cutting line and check the position of the batten before starting the cut. Check that the clamps will not foul the saw body as you make the cut.

8 To make an angled cut, loosen the wing nuts at the front and back of the soleplate and rotate the saw body to the setting you want. Lock the nuts and test the cutting angle on some scrap wood.

9 Align the left-hand edge of the wider guide notch on the front of the soleplate with the marked cutting line. Start the saw and feed the blade into the workpiece, then move the saw forward to make the cut. Keep the notch aligned with the cutting line. Remember that cutting depths are reduced when making angled cuts.

Smoothing wood

Before applying a decorative finish, you will need to sand the surface by hand or with a power sander.

Sanding by hand

The traditional way of smoothing wood is to wrap a piece of abrasive paper round a cork sanding block and to rub it along the direction of the grain. Sanding across the grain can leave scratches that are difficult to remove and can mar a clear finish. Glasspaper (generally sold as 'sandpaper') is the cheapest sheet abrasive available, but aluminium oxide abrasives cut better and last longer. Both types are sold in standard 280 x 230mm sheets.

Power sanding

Disc sanding attachments (used with a power drill) can leave tell-tale scratches. Integral power sanders give better results. Different types do different jobs. All use aluminium oxide abrasive sheets, graded as for hand abrasives.

Using a finishing sander

This sander scrubs the surface of the wood, moving its baseplate in small orbits to give a very fine, scratch-free surface finish. Large models take third-sheets (230 x 93mm) of abrasive paper; smaller models called palm sanders take quarter-sheets (115 x 70mm) or special own-brand shaped sheets. Those with a dust extraction facility use perforated sanding sheets, often attached with touch-and-close (Velcro) fastenings. Make sure the sheets you buy will fit your sander.

1 Select the correct grade of abrasive sheet for the finish you want to achieve and attach it to the sanding pad so that the holes in sheet and pad are aligned. Press it firmly into place on the pad.

2 Connect the sander to the hose of your vacuum cleaner using the adaptor provided, and switch the vacuum cleaner on. Or fit the dust bag if the tool has one.

3 Hold the tool against the surface you want to sand and switch on the power. Keep the sander moving backwards and forwards over the surface until it is smooth.

Using a belt sander

A belt sander is ideal for fast removal of material – for example, smoothing rough-sawn timber in the garden – and it will also strip paint and sand other materials such as plastic or metal if fitted with the appropriate abrasive belt. Note that there are more than a dozen different belt sizes available to fit different belt sander makes and models, so make sure you buy the correct size for your machine.

1 Release the roller tension lever and fit the belt over the rollers. Check that it is aligned with the edges of the rollers and tension the belt. Also check the tracking adjustment to ensure that the belt is positioned correctly. If it is not, it will run off the rollers in use.

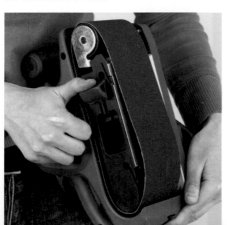

2 Fit the dust bag or connect the sander to your vacuum cleaner hose via the adaptor supplied.

3 Switch the sander on and drive it over the surface you are sanding, working only along the grain direction. Keep the tool moving, or you will gouge out more material than necessary and leave an uneven finish. Change to finer grades of belt to achieve the finish you want.

Using a detail sander

This small, orbital sander uses triangular sanding sheets attached to a matching pad, and is used for sanding into corners where an orbital sander will not reach. It does not usually have a dust bag. Some models have a rotating head that allows you to use all three corners of the sheet before replacing it; on fixed-head machines you reposition the abrasive sheet.

Shaping by hand

Most of the wood you use will be in standard sizes or a ready-machined moulding. Chisels, rasps and Surforms will help you when you need to shape wood for a particular purpose.

If you need a component that is not available as a standard size or profile, you will have to alter its cross-section or shape. For this you need a plane and a router respectively. You can cut curves with a suitable saw. Rounded ends or surfaces curved in more than one direction need another approach.

Paring with a chisel

The simplest way to form a rounded end or corner is to trim (pare) it with a chisel.

1 Mark the shape you want to cut on your workpiece. Clamp it securely on your workbench, with some scrap wood or board underneath it to protect the bench surface. Cut off the bulk of the area with a saw before you use the chisel.

2 Use a sharpened chisel (see page 58) to pare the remaining wood. Continue trimming off finer and finer shavings until you have cut back to the marked line.

3 Smooth the resulting curve with a fine rasp (see below) and then abrasive paper.

Shaping with a wood rasp

A rasp is often confused with a file, which is a metalworking tool and has parallel cutting edges machined across its blade. Rasp blades have individual raised teeth, which remove wood in the same manner as coarse abrasive paper. The tool cuts on the forward stroke. If the teeth become clogged with wood fibres as you work, clean them with a wire brush.

1 Mark the curve you want to shape on the workpiece, and clamp it securely in a vice or the jaws of your workbench.

2 Hold the handle in one hand and place the tool on the work. Steady the tip of the blade with your other hand to keep the blade flat on the surface.

3 Push the tool forwards to start shaping the wood, repeating the stroke and moving the contact point round the curve as you work to create the required shape.

4 To shape a concave curve, use a round rasp or the rounded face of a half-round rasp and work from both sides of the workpiece to prevent splintering.

Shaping with a Surform

A Surform is a rasp with a difference, having individual cutting teeth stamped out of a thin steel sheet. There are tools for different jobs, with blades that are flat, gently rounded, curved or rolled into a cylinder. The blades are replaceable.

1 Hold the tool parallel with the wood grain and push it along the wood in a series of steady strokes.

2 Clear shavings from the inside of the blade as needed. As you near the shape you want, turn the tool slightly to alter the cutting angle and produce finer shavings.

Using a plane

A bench (jack) plane about 350mm long is used to reduce the cross-section of wood from an off-the-peg size to the dimensions required. Its blade must be sharp to cut the wood cleanly (see right) and must be correctly adjusted.

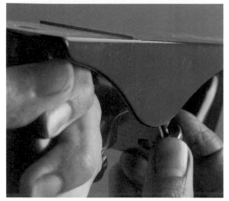

1 Sight along the soleplate of the plane to check that the blade is set square to it, and that it projects by the correct distance. Use the lateral adjustment lever behind the blade to set the cutting edge squarely, and the knurled nut between blade and handle to alter the blade projection.

2 Mark the cutting line on both faces of the workpiece and clamp it securely in your workbench. Hold the plane on the near end of the workpiece and use your free hand to grasp the front handle. Press the fingers of this hand against the side of the workpiece to guide the plane along its edge.

3 Plane from one end of the workpiece to the other in smooth, steady strokes. Let the plane run off the wood at each end of the stroke. Regularly check your progress towards the marked lines. Remove shavings from the jaws as you work.

Sharpening blades

Chisel and plane blades must be kept sharp if they are to cut well – and safely. You are more likely to force a blunt tool, with the increased risk of it slipping and injuring you or damaging the workpiece. To sharpen them you need an oilstone, a honing guide and some light machine oil.

Prepare a new oilstone for use by pouring a teaspoonful of oil onto it and smearing it over the stone. Leave it to soak in, then apply a second spoonful and repeat the process. Wipe off any excess oil with absorbent paper.

1 Clamp the blade in the honing guide, following the instructions. Check that the blade projects by the correct distance and tighten the clamping nuts fully.

2 Pour a little oil on the stone (use the fine side if it has two different faces). Move the guide up and down the stone in a figure of 8 pattern so you use as much of the surface as possible. You will wear a groove in the stone if you simply run the blade up and down the middle. Press down on the honing guide to keep the chisel tip flat against the stone.

3 Release the blade from the guide and rub its flat side back and forth across the stone to remove the curl of metal (the burr) formed on the cutting edge by the sharpening process.

Using a power planer

A power planer is useful for re-sizing work as well as jobs such as fitting new doors. Read the instructions and ensure you know how to fit and change the cutting blades.

For general bench work, use the planer in the same way as a bench plane. If you are working on a door, fit the guide fence to the planer and clamp the door on your portable workbench so you can plane the ends and edges as shown below.

1 Mark cutting lines on the workpiece, set the cutting depth on the planer and fit the fence.

2 Place the front of the soleplate against the end of the door with the fence resting on its face, and switch the tool on. Move it forwards, guiding it with both hands.

3 As you complete each pass, let the planer run off the end of the workpiece. Repeat until you reach the marked lines.

4 You can use a power planer to chamfer edges at 45°, too, by letting the groove in the soleplate run along the edge of the workpiece. Mark guide lines on each face of the work and plane down to them.

Using a router

Different bits and accessories allow you to use a router to create edge profiles, grooves and recesses in solid wood and man-made boards.

Setting up the router

1 To fit your selected cutting bit, use the spanner and locking pin provided. Place the router on its side and lock the chuck (called the collet) with the pin. Loosen the collet with the spanner and insert the bit as far as it will go. Tighten the collet fully and remove the locking pin.

2 To set the routing depth, stand the router on the workbench and undo the winged nut securing the depth rod so it is free to move. Loosen the side handle, press the body of the router down until the bit touches the bench surface and tighten the handle again.

3 Read off the value indicated on the depth scale and add the required routing depth to it. Set the pointer on the depth rod to this combined figure and tighten the winged nut below the scale. Loosen the side handle and allow the router body to rise up on its springs. Check that the routing depth is correct by making a test cut on some scrap wood.

4 If the machine has a dust extractor facility, fit the adaptor and connect it to the hose of your vacuum cleaner.

Routing an edge profile

The router cutter rotates counter-clockwise when viewed from above the tool. Always feed the cutter into the wood from the right, so it is turning into the wood it is about to cut away. If you work in the opposite direction, the speed of the machine may wrench it from your grasp and damage your work.

1 Select the cutter you want to use and fit it in the collet. Set the cutting depth required. Clamp the work securely to your workbench, checking that the clamps will not impede the router.

2 Rest the edge of the soleplate on top of the workpiece. Switch the router on, press the body down on its springs and guide it sideways into the edge you are shaping. Cut in until the guide pin touches the edge of the workpiece.

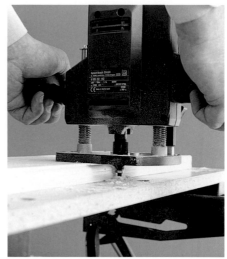

3 Start the motor and move the router forwards slowly to cut the groove. Keep the fence pressed against the edge of the workpiece. Let the cutter run out at the end of the groove and switch off.

3 Move the router slowly forwards, with the baseplate flat on the surface of the workpiece. Let the cutter run off at the far end of the cut and switch off the power.

Using a guide fence

To machine a groove parallel with the edge of the workpiece, fit the guide fence to the router soleplate using the guide plates and winged screws. Mark the position of the groove on the workpiece and set the cutting depth required.

1 Place the router on the workpiece with the cutter aligned with the marked line. Move the fence in against the edge of the workpiece and tighten the securing screws.

2 Position the router soleplate on the end of the workpiece with the fence pressed against its edge. Start the motor, loosen the side handle and press the router body down to the pre-set cutting depth. Tighten the handle again.

Using a guide batten

If you want to cut grooves further in from the edge of the workpiece than the fence will allow, use a guide batten instead. Clamp it across the workpiece and guide the flat side of the router soleplate against it as you machine the groove. Check that the clamps will not impede the movement of the router.

Choosing router bits

Bits for DIY routers usually have 6mm diameter shafts and tungsten carbide cutting tips. Grooving cutters are plain, while shaping (edge) cutters have a guide wheel that runs against the edge of the workpiece and stops the bit from cutting too deeply. You can buy bits singly but it is better to buy a set with a storage case.

Making joints

The type of joint will depend on how strong you want it to be and its appearance. This section will help you to choose the appropriate method.

Basic joints

Butt joints These are the easiest joints to make. They are formed by aligning the two components (such as the sides of a box) so that the edge of one overlaps the end of the other. Butt joints can also be used to join wood edge to edge – to make a table top, for example. There are several options for joining the components:

• Fix the corner joint together with nails or screws and strengthen with wood glue.
• Reinforce a corner or edge joint with hardwood dowels or oval-shaped slips of compressed wood called biscuits.
• Use one of the ingenious assembly fittings originally designed for flat-pack furniture.
• Use a metal angle bracket or a corrugated fastener (below), although these remain visible unless you take steps to hide them.

Halving joints These are made by cutting away half of each component so they fit together neatly. The joint is stronger than a butt joint because the parts interlock. If the joint is also glued, it is even stronger because the glued contact area between the parts is bigger. The joint is usually nailed or screwed. Halving joints are used mainly in frames, and components can be joined in L, T or X shapes. The last two – called tee halving joints and cross halving joints respectively – need a slot cut in one or both components.

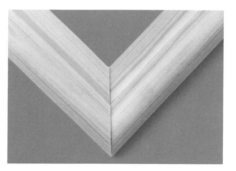

Mitre joints Butt joints that meet at a 45° angle are called mitre joints. They are used mainly in frames, where the appearance of the corner joint is important – in a picture frame, for example, or where the architrave mouldings round a door opening meet. Like butt joints they can be nailed, screwed, dowel-jointed or biscuit-jointed, and are usually glued as well.

Using a try square to mark up joints

The most important feature of any woodworking joint is that it should be square, and the try square is the tool to use for checking this. You also need a try square for marking cutting lines at 90°, both when cutting wood to length and when marking out halving joints.

1 Mark where you want to cut your workpiece to length. Hold the stock of the try square against its edge at the mark, with the blade across the width, and mark the line with a trimming knife or pencil.

2 Turn the workpiece through 90°, align the try square with the marked line on its face and mark the line on its edge. Repeat the process to continue the marked line all the way round the workpiece. This continuous line will help you to cut the wood squarely to length.

2 Hold the block against one face of the workpiece and mark the edge with the pin. Then hold it against the opposite face and repeat the mark. If they coincide, the gauge is correctly set. If they do not, move the block slightly and repeat the process until they do. Tighten the screw fully.

3 To mark out a corner halving joint, clamp the two pieces together and check with the try square that they are at 90° to each other. Mark the edge of each piece on the face of the other.

3 Hold the block against the face of each component in turn, and slide it along so the pin marks the halving line on each edge of each component, extending to the end from the cutting line you marked with the try square.

4 Separate the two pieces and use the try square to continue the marked lines onto the edge of each piece.

Using a marking gauge

To mark out a halving joint, you need a marking gauge. This enables you to mark the thickness of the wood you want to cut away from each component.

1 Loosen the thumbscrew on the block and slide it along the beam so the pin is approximately half the thickness of the workpiece away from the block. Tighten the screw.

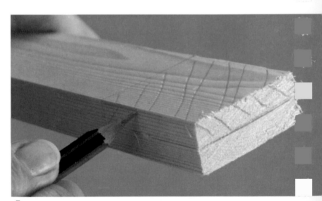

4 Join the edge marks across the end grain of each component. Then cross-hatch the area to be cut away in pencil on each component, ready for the joint to be cut.

Making corner halving joints

Once you have marked out the two components, you can cut and assemble the joint. You need a tenon saw and some wood adhesive (or a glue gun).

1 Clamp each component on its edge and, starting the cut at an angle, begin to saw along the grain.

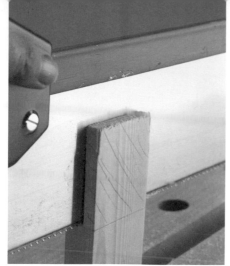

2 Then complete the cut down to the shoulder marks, holding the saw blade at right-angles to the workpiece.

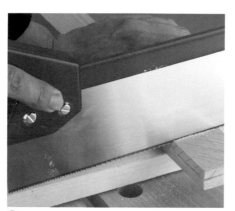

3 Using a bench hook to steady the workpiece, cut carefully across the width to form the shoulder.

4 Squirt some adhesive onto the cut faces of one component and assemble the joint. Clamp it for maximum bond strength, with cardboard or scrap wood between the clamp jaws and the workpieces to prevent dents. Use your try square to check that the joint is a perfect right angle. Wipe away excess adhesive with a damp cloth.

Making T-halving joints

As with a corner halving joint, use the two components you wish to join to mark the outline of the joint.

1 Clamp the two components together, check that they are at right angles and mark the edges of each component on the face of the other one.

2 Use a marking gauge to mark the joint thickness on the edge of each component. Cut the piece forming the leg of the tee in the same way as for a corner halving joint.

3 Using a tenon saw, make two parallel cuts on the waste side of the marks on the piece forming the cross-bar of the tee. Saw down to the halfway line. Then make several more cuts to the same depth within the waste area (below).

4 Clamp the workpiece securely and, using a sharp chisel, begin to chisel out the waste wood between the outer saw cuts.

5 Work from opposite sides in turn so as to avoid splintering, until the base of the notch is flat and is level with the halfway lines on the edges.

6 Test the fit of the two components, and shave away any excess wood with your chisel if necessary.

7 Glue and assemble the joint as for a corner halving joint.

Making mitre joints

You can cut mitre joints freehand after marking the cutting angles with a combination square, or by using a protractor and ruler. Alternatively, you can use a mitre box to guide the saw.

1 Mark the joint positions on each component. Set the cutting angle to 45° by rotating the saw's baseplate, then lock it.

2 Clamp the workpiece in place on the base of the mitre saw and lower the saw blade to check that the cut will be aligned with the mark. Then make the cut. Repeat for the other component of the joint.

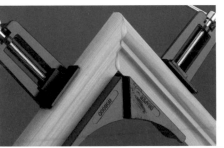

3 Apply adhesive to one mitred end and assemble the joint. Check that it is square, set it aside and leave it until the adhesive has set. You can reinforce the joint by driving a panel pin or a screw in from each side of the joint, or you can drill holes in each mitred face to take dowels. Special cramps are available that will hold the joint accurately while the adhesive sets. You can also reinforce mitre joints with biscuits.

Making biscuit joints

You need a power tool called a biscuit jointer to cut the slots for the biscuits in the two components. Follow the instructions supplied with the tool to cut the slots. Then squirt woodworking adhesive into the slots, insert the biscuits and assemble the joint. Clamp the joint until the adhesive has set.

Making dowel joints

The positions of the dowel holes must be carefully matched in the two components being joined. Use a drill bit that matches readily available sizes of hardwood dowel – commonly 6 or 8mm in diameter. It's a good idea to use a drill stand or a dowelling jig to ensure that the holes are drilled at precise right angles to the face of the workpiece, and to the correct depth.

1 Use a combination square to mark a centre line on the end or edge of the first component to be drilled. Mark the dowel positions on this line and corresponding marks on the second component.

2 Drill a hole at each cross in the first component, making the holes a little deeper than half the length of the dowel. Use a drill stand or clamp the dowelling jig to the workpiece and use it to guide the drill bit.

3 Squeeze some wood glue into the holes and insert the dowels. Drill the dowel holes in the second component, ready for the joint to be assembled.

4 Check the alignment of the two components before squeezing some glue into the holes and assembling the joint.

5 Use a wooden mallet to knock the joint together. Wipe away any surplus adhesive with a damp cloth.

HELPFUL TIP

When making dowel joints, one way to ensure accurate holes is to drill dowel holes in one of the pieces to join, then put specially designed metal marker pins in the holes. Offer up the pieces in exactly the position you want and knock them together firmly. The markers will leave indentations in the other piece of wood, ready for perfectly-matched holes to be drilled in it.

Self-assembly fixings for flat-pack furniture

When you buy an item of flat-pack furniture, it comes with fixing holes already drilled and special types of fixing to enable you to assemble it yourself easily and with the minimum number of tools. Often all you need is a special spanner or hex key supplied with the unit. Here are some of the most common fixings that you are likely to encounter.

Many of these are also available to buy separately so that you can use them when making your own units. Always use fittings in pairs and use a steel ruler, not a tape measure, when marking where to drill – it is essential for drill holes to be accurately positioned if the unit is to be square when assembled.

Two block fitting (Lok joint)

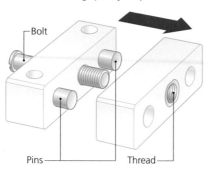

The joint consists of two plastic blocks and is normally used to join two sections of cupboard together, such as a side to the base. One of the blocks is screwed to the base and the other to the side into pre-drilled holes; a bolt is then screwed in to hold the two sections firmly together. One of the advantages of this type of fixing is that it can be disassembled and reassembled whenever necessary with no loss of strength.

Plastic corner block

One of the simplest of the fittings that is often found in flat pack furniture. Plastic corner blocks hold two panels together at a

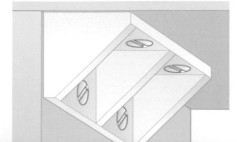

perfect right angle. As screws are driven into the carcase material, this fitting cannot be taken apart and reused without compromising its strength.

Dowels

Dowels are best for joints that are not to be taken apart once assembled. Usually about 25–30mm long, they are glued in place.

Like the majority of the fixings used in flat-pack furniture they are tapped into factory-made pre-drilled holes. Although simple they are very effective and give a strong concealed joint.

Dowel and screw fitting

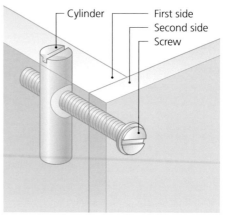

These are one of the most popular joints used in flat-pack furniture. The cylinder is inserted into a factory-made pre-drilled hole in one side of the cabinet. A machine screw is then inserted into a hole in the other side until it meets the cylinder. The two components are tightened with a screwdriver until both sides of the cabinet pull together. The slot in the head of the cylinder part of the fitting allows you to align it so that it will receive the screw (below). Although it is possible to over-tighten these fittings they do hold very securely and can be repeatedly taken apart with no loss of strength.

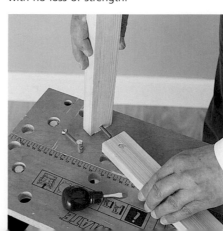

Cam lock fittings

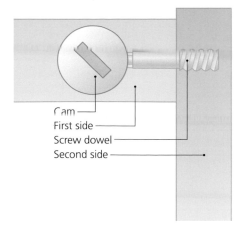

Cam —
First side
Screw dowel
Second side

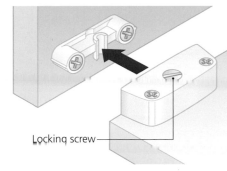

Locking screw

This cam fitting is similar to the Lok joint. The two parts of the joint are screwed into separate panels. The two panels are then brought together and the screw is turned through 90° to lock the joint.

Like the dowel and screw fitting, this fastening is for joining two planks or panels together. The cam is dropped into a shallow recess on the face of one part and a screw with a pronounced head or a steel screw dowel is driven into a pre-drilled hole in the other part to be joined.

The head of the screw passes through a clearance hole in the first part and into the cam. Turning the cam 90° clockwise tightens the joint.

Dowel and bush fitting

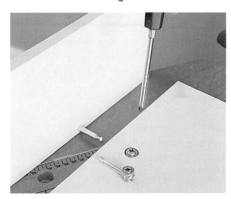

This fitting consists of a zinc alloy bush and a steel dowel. Screw the dowel into the face of one board so that when it is butt-jointed with the second board it will align with the hole drilled in the second board's edge. The dowel reaches the bush through that hole and is locked in place by turning the grub screw in the bush.

Some cam fittings come with the peg attached to a disc the same size as the cam. Both components slot into pre-drilled holes in the panels to be joined.

Another variation on this type of fitting replaces the peg with a special moulding like a wall plug. This is pushed into a hole drilled in the edge of the second board. A pin is driven into the plug and the fitting is assembled as before.

Housing and bolt fitting

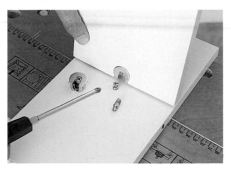

A bolt screws into the side panel of a cupboard or shelf unit and fits into the housing, which slots into a hole drilled in the underside of the shelf. These fittings are useful for strengthening shelves in an existing unit or for adding extra shelves.

Assembling flat-pack furniture

Whether you are putting together a simple bookshelf, a more complex piece of flat-pack furniture, or an entire fitted kitchen there are some simple rules to follow that will help to guarantee success.

Most flat-pack units consist of a series of panels that are fitted together to create a basic box. Extras, such as doors, shelves and internal fittings, are then added to this to complete the job. Always work in a logical order, following the instructions that came with the unit.

Tools *Selection of screwdrivers; perhaps a hammer; perhaps a set of hex keys.*

1 Unpack the kit and lay out all the components, including the assembly fittings and any other items of hardware such as hinges, handles and feet. Lay the panels on a soft surface, such as a carpet, or the box they were supplied in to minimise scratches.

2 Identify all the parts, using the instructions, and check that you have the right number of fixings – there is usually a numbered checklist included with the instructions. If any appear to be missing, look inside the packaging to see if any are loose inside. If not, return the complete unit to the store and ask for a replacement.

3 Start with the base panel, adding any fixed feet first of all. Build tall units, such as

WHEN GLUING IS BEST

If you know that you will not be taking the furniture apart again at some time in the future, consider using adhesive on wood-to-wood joints for a sturdier finished piece. Ordinary white carpenters' PVA adhesive is ideal. Use a damp rag to wipe off any excess adhesive that squeezes from the joints.

bookshelves or wardrobes, on their backs to make the assembly manageable. If the unit has castors or wheels, fit these last or the unit will move about as you work.

4 Connect the first side panel to the base panel. The simplest units have pre-drilled holes through which you can drive screws supplied with the furniture.

5 Many fixings come with cover discs that match the colour of the wood or veneer of the finished item. These make a tidy job of disguising the fixings once the furniture is complete. They can be prised out of their holes if you need access to the fixings to dismantle the furniture.

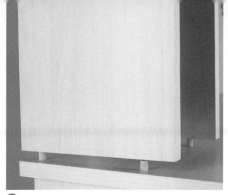

6 Another simple solution is to use dowel fixings. Glue the dowels and place them in the holes provided and then offer up the corresponding panel. If you need to, hammer from above, being sure to protect the workpiece with some scrap timber.

7 Many units use a combination of glued dowels and cam or dowel and bush fixings (see pages 66–67). To fit cam fixings to lock onto the screwed pegs, use your thumb to push the cam locks into the large holes pre-drilled for them, making sure that the arrow on the fitting points towards the holes on the raw outside edge of the workpiece. The dowels fit into these holes, so if the locks don't face in the right direction the fixings will not work.

8 Screw the dowels into the holes in the corresponding panels of the unit. Bring the two panels together and use the special key supplied as part of the kit to tighten the cam locks so that they grip securely.

HELPFUL TIP

Much flat-pack and self-assembly furniture comes with a hexagonal assembly key and every unit comes with a set of instructions. When you have finished putting the piece of furniture together, tape the key and instructions securely to the back, so that you will always have them handy if you ever have to move, dismantle or adjust your furniture.

9 Once you have a three-sided box, locate the back panel if there is one in the grooves in the side panels and slide it into place. Finish the box with the top panel.

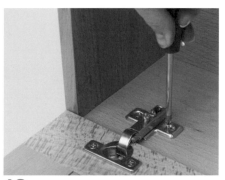

10 Follow the instructions with the unit to add any doors. They will be hung on some form of spring-loaded hinges, and the fitting and fixing holes will all be pre-drilled in the doors and cabinet sides. Fit the hinge body to the door and the mounting plate to the cabinet sides, then connect the two with the short machine screws and adjust them so they hang squarely.

11 Add any shelves, door handles and other internal or external fittings. Double-check that all the assembly fittings are tight, and that you do not have any parts left over. Finally, fit wheels or castors if these are part of the kit.

SAFETY TIP

Tall pieces of furniture, such as bookshelves or wardrobes, should be secured to the wall at the top of the unit, using a bracket or restraining strap. Without them a fully loaded unit could topple over on a child climbing on it or clambering inside.

Decorating
your home

Hanging standard wallpaper

Papering the walls is normally the last stage in decorating. Once you have mastered the simple techniques, the job is quick and easy.

Tools *Pasting table; bucket; brush; paper-hanger's brush; steel tape measure; plumb line; pencil; wallpaper scissors and small scissors; sponge; seam roller.*

Materials *Size; wallpaper paste; wallpaper.*

Before you start Size bare walls to prevent them from absorbing paste from the wallcovering. Size also makes the surface slippery so that the covering can be slid into place. You can either buy size or use a dilute form of the paste you plan to use to hang the wall covering.

Apply size with the paste brush or a short-pile paint roller to cover the whole surface and spread the size evenly. If the size gets onto painted woodwork, wipe it off immediately with a damp cloth.

Cutting paper to length

1 Take a roll of paper and check which way the pattern goes. Decide where definite motifs should be in relation to the top of the wall.

2 With a steel tape, measure the wall height down to the top of the skirting board. Add an extra 100mm for trimming at the top and bottom.

3 Unroll the paper on the pasting table, pattern-side down, measure the length and draw a line with a pencil and straight-edge across the back.

4 Cut along the line with a pair of long-bladed scissors.

5 Turn the paper over, unroll the next length and match the pattern by placing it edge to edge with the first length. Using the cut length as a measuring guide, cut off the second length.

Continue in this way until several lengths are ready for pasting. Number them on the back so that you know the hanging order, and note which end is the top.

Pasting the paper

1 Lay the cut lengths on the pasting table, pattern side down.

2 Position the top piece of paper so that all the spare paper hangs off the table to the right. If you are left-handed, reverse all the following paper-hanging procedures.

3 Adjust the paper so that the long edge aligns with the edge of the table.

4 Load the paste brush and wipe off excess paste by dragging the brush across the string on the bucket.

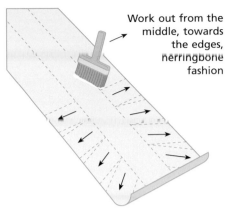

Work out from the middle, towards the edges, herringbone fashion

5 Brush the paste down the centre of the paper, then out to the edges. If any paste gets onto the table, wipe it off with a damp cloth.

6 Check that all the paper is evenly covered with paste, especially the edges. Holding the left-hand edge, loosely fold the paper over – paste side to paste side – to about the centre of the length.

7 Slide the paper to the left of the table so that the pasted part hangs off the edge.

8 Paste the right-hand end of the paper as you did the left, brushing in a herringbone pattern until the paper is all pasted.

9 Fold the paper over – without creasing it – so the top and bottom edges meet.

10 Leave the pasted paper to soak for as long as the manufacturer recommends. Thin paper and vinyl will be ready to hang almost immediately but heavier materials need to be left for 10 to 15 minutes.

Hanging the first length

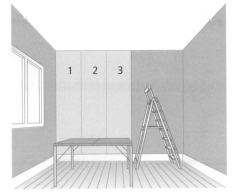

Start hanging the paper on a wall next to the window wall and work away from the light source, so that any slight overlaps will not cast shadows, which make the joins obvious. If there is more than one window in the room, treat the larger one as the main light source.

1 Pencil a mark near the top of the wall, 480mm out from the corner, so that enough paper will turn onto the window wall.

2 Hold the plumb line to the mark and let the bob hang free about 1.2m down the wall. When the bob settles, make another pencil mark directly behind the string. Check the distance to the corner all the way down the wall. If it is greater than 480mm at any point because the corner is not true, not enough paper will turn. So make the top measurement shorter, use the plumb line again and draw new pencil marks.

3 Carry the pasted length to the wall and release the top fold gently, holding it at both sides. Do not let the lower half drop suddenly – it may tear, or stretch and cause matching problems.

4 Hold the top right corner against the wall so that the right-hand edge of the paper aligns with the pencil mark. Make sure about 50mm of excess paper is left at the top of the wall for trimming.

5 Keep the left edge of the paper off the wall while you align the right-hand edge on the lower pencil mark.

6 Once the right edge is in place, smooth the paper with your hand or paperhanging brush diagonally up until the top left corner of the paper is on the wall.

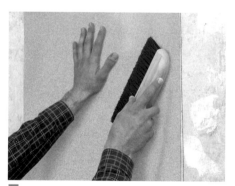

7 Let go of the paper and smooth out the top half of the length with the paper-hanging brush, working from the centre outwards. Make sure the paper stays on the pencil mark.

8 Release the lower fold. Brush down the centre of the length, then out to the edges as you did when pasting, ensuring that any bubbles are brushed out. Dab down the edges with the tip of the brush or a dry, clean cloth made into a pad.

9 With the length in place, run the back of a pair of scissors along the paper where it meets the skirting board to crease it.

10 Pull the paper gently away from the wall and cut along the crease, with the underside of the paper facing you. Brush the trimmed edge back in place. Repeat this process at the top of the length.

Alternatively A trimming guide gives a neater edge. Slide the guide under the paper and cut off the excess with a trimming knife. The blade must be razor-sharp or it will tear the damp wallpaper. If you feel the knife pulling at the paper, change the blade.

Hanging the next lengths

1 Hang the second length of paper to the right of the piece on the wall, following the same procedure but without using the plumb line. Match the top section of the left edge of the new length with the length on the wall, then run your hand diagonally up and to the right to press the top of the paper to the wall.

2 Smooth out the paper from the centre with the paperhanging brush.

3 Release the lower fold, check that the edges match and continue to brush over the paper. Trim top and bottom as before.

4 With two or three pieces hung, run the seam roller lightly down the joins of smooth papers. Do not press down the edges of textured materials or you will flatten the pattern.

HELPFUL TIP

Push a tipless matchstick into each hole or wallplug, leaving it just proud of the surface. Ease through the paper to show where fittings are.

Wallpapering around corners

All rooms have internal corners and often external ones as well – on a chimney breast, for example.

External corners

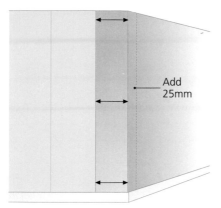

Add 25mm

Never try to turn more than 25mm around an external corner – the turned paper is likely to slant and look crooked. This technique can be applied to rounded walls as well as right-angled corners.

1 Paper the wall until there is less than one width to the corner.

2 Measure the distance between the edge of the last hung length and the corner, at the top, middle and bottom of the wall. Add 25mm to allow for the turn and cut the paper to this size.

3 Hang the length as far as the corner and take the overlap around onto the next wall. Smooth away any bubbles with the paperhanging brush.

4 Hang the offcut from the first length next to the paper on the wall, matching the pattern and butting the joins. Continue to hang lengths until you reach the internal corner. Before you paper the next wall, use the plumb line to get a vertical starting point. If the walls in the room are very out of true, it is easier to overlap rather than butt the joins – especially if the paper has a vertical pattern.
   Take the pasted paper around the corner. Deduct 25mm from the width of the offcut and mark pencil lines this far away from the corner, using the plumb line to get a true vertical. Hang the paper, overlapping the piece turned round the corner.

Internal corners

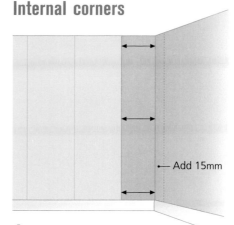

Add 15mm

1 Measure the distance between the last length you have hung and the corner at the top, middle and bottom of the wall. Note the widest distance and add 15mm to allow for the turn onto the next wall.

2 Cut a length to this width. Keep the offcut for papering the first section of the adjoining wall.

3 Paste and hang the length. Take the overlap onto the next wall. Use the brush to smooth the paper well into the corner. If creases form, tear the paper – but cut vinyl – and overlap the torn pieces so that they lie flat.

4 Measure the offcut and hang the plumb line this distance away from the corner to find a vertical. Make pencil marks behind the line at intervals down the wall.

5 Hang the offcut with the right-hand edge aligning with the pencil marks. The length will overlap the paper turned from the previous wall. If the paper is patterned, match the two pieces as closely as possible. Use special overlap adhesive with vinyls.

Wallpapering in awkward places

Light switches or sockets

1 Turn off the electricity at the mains. Hang the paper from the top of the wall down as far as the switch or socket.

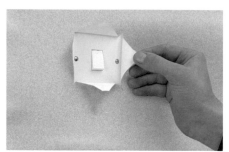

2 Cut the paper to the corners of the switch and pull back the flaps.

3 Partially unscrew the switch cover and pull it about 5mm away from the wall.

4 Trim away excess paper so that about 3mm of paper will sit behind the cover.

5 Gently ease the switch cover through the hole in the paper.

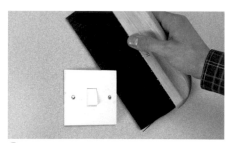

6 Push the paper behind the switch cover with a piece of flat wood, then brush the paper flat, smoothing away any air bubbles.

7 Hang the remainder of the length. Tighten the switch cover screws and turn the electricity supply back on.

SAFETY TIP

Never put metallic or foil wall coverings behind light switches. They may conduct electricity.

Radiators

1 Tuck the paper in behind the radiator until you reach the supporting bracket. Hang the next piece over the radiator, brushing it flat as far down as possible.

2 Use a pencil to mark the position of the wall bracket on the back of the paper and make a vertical cut in the paper from the bottom edge to the top of the bracket.

3 Feed the paper down behind the radiator and smooth down with a radiator roller. Trim it at the skirting board. Alternatively, if the radiator overhangs the skirting board, save paper by trimming it off 150mm below the top of the radiator.

4 Sponge any paste off the radiator before it dries.

Fireplaces

1 Cut the lengths of paper that are to go round the fireplace roughly to size before applying paste, so that you do not have to cope with a lot of pasted paper when trimming. Leave a margin of at least 25mm for trimming in situ.

2 Paste and hang paper, then mark the outline of the fireplace on the paper using the back of a scissor blade.

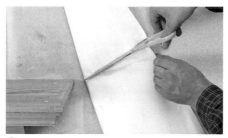

3 Peel a little of the paper away from the wall so you can work comfortably. Cut along the marked outline. Use small, sharp scissors if there are lots of small cuts; otherwise, use paperhanging scissors. If the trimming takes some time and the paste is beginning to dry, apply a little more paste to the wall, rather than to the paper.

4 Smooth the paper in place all around the fireplace, using the points of bristles of a paperhanging brush to push the paper into awkward corners. Continue down to the skirting board.

Door frames

1 When you get to the door, hang a pasted, full-length strip next to the last length, allowing the strip to flap over the door. Press the paper against the top corner of the architrave. Make a diagonal cut from the loose edge to the architrave top corner.

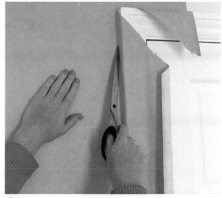

2 Brush paper into the angles between the wall and the architrave above and beside the door. Use scissors to crease the paper.

3 Trim off the excess paper along the side of the door, working from the bottom upwards. Then cut off the waste paper above the door opening.

4 Using a paperhanging brush, press the trimmed edges back into place against the edges of the architrave. Then cut the top edge of the length to fit at ceiling level, and the bottom edge at the skirting board.

5 You will probably need to hang a short length of wallpaper above the door. Use scissors to crease the paper into the angle between wall and ceiling, then into the angle between wall and architrave. Trim the paper to fit. When cutting above the architrave, leave the paper slightly over-long so that it covers the top edge.

6 Repeat steps 1 to 4 to hang another full-length strip at the opposite side of the door opening, again letting it overlap the door architrave so you can mark the corner and cut the waste paper away. Brush the cut edges back into place, then carry on papering the rest of the wall.

Recessed windows

1 When you reach a window recess, hang a full length drop of paper so that it overlaps the opening. If the overlap is large, you may need a helper to support the weight of the pasted paper.

2 Make a neat, horizontal scissor cut level with the top edge of the recess.

3 Make a second cut level with the top surface of the window sill.

4 If the flap of paper that you have created is enough to cover the depth of the recess, crease it into the angle with a paperhanging brush. If it is not deep enough to reach the window frame, cut and paste a strip a little wider than the gap and hang it on the side of the reveal, matching it to the pattern, if there is one.

5 Run scissors along the crease to make a defined cutting line. Peel back the paper and make a neat scissor cut to trim off the excess. Brush the paper back into place.

6 Cut a piece of wallpaper long enough to reach from the ceiling to the top of the window, into the recess and up to the frame, with extra for trimming. Hang this next to the previous full-length strip, and brush into the recess. Trim at ceiling level and where paper meets the frame. Repeat until you need another full-length piece.

7 Paper under the windowsill. Measure from the underside of the sill to the top of the skirting board, then add 50mm or so for trimming. Cut strips of paper to this length and hang them under the window, matching the pattern if necessary. Repeat to cover the rest of the wall below the window opening, stopping when the next piece needed is a full-length one.

8 Check that the last piece hung above the window is in line with the last piece below it by hanging a plumb line. If it is not, measure the discrepancy at its widest point and subtract this from the width of a piece of paper. Mark a plumb line on the wall to the right of the window at this distance from the edge of the overhanging piece of paper.

9 Hang the next whole length. Butt it up to the previous pieces if they were in line, or position its right hand edge level with the plumb line you have drawn if the paper above and below the window was misaligned.

10 There will be a gap in each top corner of the reveal. Cut a strip of paper the width of the gap at top left, but 50mm deeper than the recess. Position the paper over the gap, allowing about 25mm to turn up at the front edge onto the wall above, matching the pattern, if there is one.

11 Use a trimming knife and straight-edge to cut through both the patch and the paper above it, 15mm above the edge of the recess. Peel away the offcuts from each piece and then press the edges flat for an invisible butt join. Cover the gap in the other corner of the reveal in the same way.

Tiling a wall

You can set out and centre tiles for a splashback by eye. On a wall, a simple aid called a tiling gauge makes the setting out much easier.

Half-tiling a wall to a height of about 1.2m is popular in bathrooms. If the wall is unobstructed, the centring rule is simple to apply. Each row should have cut tiles of equal width at each end (unless a row of whole tiles fills the available space exactly). Each column will have a whole tile at the top and a cut tile at the bottom.

You may be tempted to save work and start each column with a whole tile at floor or skirting board level, but the floor or skirting board may not be truly level and using it as a baseline will gradually force the tile rows and columns off square.

Using guide battens

The secret of success is to use a horizontal timber guide batten fixed to the wall beneath the bottom edge of the lowest row of whole tiles. Position it so that the gap to be filled between this row and the floor or skirting board is about three-quarters of a tile width.

You have to place all the whole tiles on the wall before you can fit any cut tiles at the ends of the rows. It is therefore a good idea to add a vertical guide batten at one side of the area, to ensure that the columns of tiles are all precisely vertical. Once all the whole tiles have been placed, remove the battens so the cut tiles can be measured, cut and fixed in place.

Using a tiling gauge

1 Measure the width of the wall to be tiled and mark the centre point. Hold the tile gauge horizontally, with one end less than a tile width from a corner and align a joint mark with the centre line. If the gap at the end of the gauge is between one-third and two-thirds of a tile wide, you have a satisfactory tile layout. Mark the wall in line with the end of the gauge. This indicates where the vertical guide batten will be fixed.

2 If the gap is narrow, or is almost a whole tile wide, it will be difficult to cut tiles to fit. You will get a better layout by moving the gauge along by half a tile width. Do this, then mark the wall in line with the end of the gauge to indicate where to fix the vertical guide batten.

3 Hold the gauge vertically to assess where the top of the tiled area will finish. Move it up so the bottom of the gauge is about three-quarters of a tile width above the floor or skirting board. Mark the wall at a joint mark to indicate the top of the tiled area. Make another mark level with the bottom of the gauge to indicate the level of the horizontal guide batten.

Fixing the battens

You now have pencil marks on the wall indicating the level of the lowest row of whole tiles and also the edge of the column of whole tiles nearest the corner.

1 Fix the horizontal guide batten first, using a spirit level to get it truly horizontal. If you are tiling more than one wall, fix guide battens to each wall and check that they are precisely aligned with each other.

2 Use a spirit level to mark a true vertical line down to the horizontal guide batten from the end mark you made on the wall with your tiling gauge.

3 Fix a vertical guide batten at this point, long enough to reach up to the top of the area to be tiled. Secure the battens with masonry nails on solid walls and with wire nails on timber-framed partitions. Leave the nail heads projecting by about 10mm so they can be pulled out easily when it is time to remove the battens.

Fixing the tiles

With the setting-out complete and the guide battens fixed, you can start to place the whole tiles on the wall. Put down a dust sheet to catch stray blobs of adhesive, unpack your tiles and spacers.

Tools *Notched spreader; stripping knife; damp cloth.*

Materials *Tiles; tile adhesive; spacers.*

1 Scoop some adhesive from the tub with your spreader and spread it on the wall in a band a little more than one tile wide. The notches form ridges in the adhesive that will be compressed to an even thickness as you place the tiles.

2 Place the first tile in the angle between the guide battens. Rest its lower edge on the horizontal batten, then press it into the adhesive. Check that its edge is against the vertical batten.

3 Place more tiles along the row, fitting a spacer between them, until you reach the corner. Press the spacers at the top corners into the adhesive so they will be covered when you grout. At the bottom corners, push one leg of each spacer into the gap between the tiles; these will be pulled out when the batten is removed.

4 Hold the edge of your tiling gauge across the faces of the tiles to check that they are flush with each other.

5 Apply another band of adhesive and place the second row of tiles. Align the bottom edge of each one between the spacers in the row below before pressing it into place. Then fit spacers between the top corners as before.

6 When you have placed the topmost row of tiles, scrape off any excess adhesive from the wall with a stripping knife and wipe off the remaining traces with a damp cloth.

7 Allow the adhesive to set for 24 hours. Then prise out the nails that are holding the guide battens in place, taking care not to dislodge the tiles. Measure and cut individual tiles to fit the width of the remaining gaps and butter some adhesive onto the back with your spreader.

8 Fit spacers into the gaps between the rows of whole tiles. Then fit the cut pieces, one at a time, into the gap between the spacers. Press the cut tile into place so its face is flush with its neighbour. Repeat the process to measure, cut and fit the remaining cut tiles at both ends of each row. Then cut tiles to fill the gap between the bottom row of whole tiles and the skirting board or floor.

POSITIONING TILES AROUND A WINDOW

Tiles look best if they are centred around a window. Use a tiling gauge to span the window and adjust its position until there is an equal width of tile on either side. Mark the wall to indicate the outer edge of the tiles that will need to be cut. Drop a plumb line through the first of the lines to transfer the mark to the horizontal batten at the bottom of the wall. Work from this mark towards the corner of the room, measuring full tile widths and grout joints to determine the position of the last whole tile in each row. Fix the vertical batten to the wall at this point.

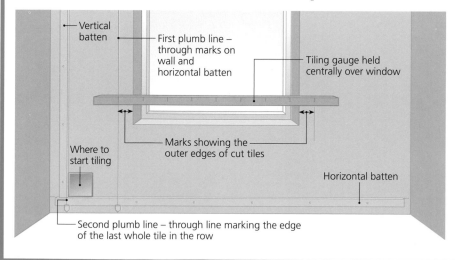

Vertical batten

First plumb line – through marks on wall and horizontal batten

Tiling gauge held centrally over window

Marks showing the outer edges of cut tiles

Where to start tiling

Horizontal batten

Second plumb line – through line marking the edge of the last whole tile in the row

TILE ADHESIVE AND GROUT

All-in-one, ready-mixed, waterproof tile adhesive and grout is the ideal choice for most tiling jobs. One 10-litre tub will cover an area of 10–12m².

Separate grouts and adhesives You can also buy adhesive and grout separately, ready-mixed or in powder form to mix with water. Mixing your own allows you to add pigment to colour the grout, but it is crucial to measure accurately to get a consistent colour over several batches. Powder products are cheaper than ready-mixed ones.

Sealing joints Use flexible mastic, not grout, to seal the joints between tiles and bathroom fittings or kitchen worktops. Use flexible mastic also to fill internal corners between tiles and where tiles meet skirting boards or architrave.

Cutting tiles to fit

Tiling a splashback is easy – you probably won't even have to cut a tile. But if you are tiling a whole wall, you will encounter various obstacles.

Tools *Chinagraph pencil; steel rule; platform tile cutter; tile saw; tile nibbler; pencil; G-cramp.*

Materials *Tiles; adhesive.*

Finishing a row

1 When you reach the end of a row, place the final tile over the previous tile and butt it up to the corner. Allow for the width of a grout joint and mark the cutting line.

2 Use a platform tile cutter to make a neat straight cut. Score the tile with the cutting wheel then use the lever to snap the tile along the line. Position the tile on the wall with the cut edge into the corner.

3 Measure the final tile in each row separately. Few walls are perfectly square, so your measurements are unlikely to be the same all the way up.

Taking a sliver off a tile

1 Platform tile cutters will not make fine cuts, less than 15mm wide. Use a hand-held tile scorer and steel straightedge. Score the tile much more deeply than you would for an ordinary cut – you need to cut right through the glaze in order to get a clean break.

2 Nibble away at the sliver of tile that is being removed, using a tile nibbler. Smooth any sharp edges with a tile file.

Cutting a curved line

1 Cut a piece of paper to the size of a tile to make a template to fit around the curved object.

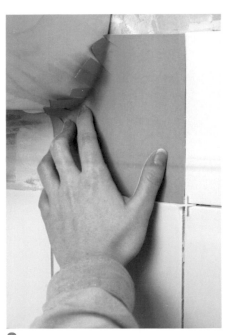

2 Make a series of cuts in the edge that will butt up to the obstacle. Press the tongues against the obstacle so that the creases define its outline.

3 Use the paper as a guide to transfer the curved line with a chinagraph pencil onto the glazed tile surface.

4 Clamp the tile face-up to a workbench, protecting the glaze with a board offcut sandwiched between tile and cramp. Cut along the marked line with a tile saw. Work slowly and with as little pressure as possible to avoid chipping the glaze. File away any excess if necessary to get a perfect fit.

POWER CUTS FOR TILES

If you have a craft drill, such as a Dremel, you can use its tile-cutting attachment to make holes in tiles. Mark the cutting line as described above, but don't split the tile in two until after you have made the hole. Cut out the circle you have marked then split the tile and fit it in place.

Making holes

1 When you tile around plumbing – in a shower, for example – you may need to make holes in the tiles to allow pipes to run through. Offer up the tile from the side and from below, and mark each edge in line with the centre of the pipe. Draw straight lines to extend the marks: where they intersect is the pipe centre. Trace round an offcut of pipe – or a coin or other round object of about the same diameter – to mark a cutting line at this point.

2 Cut the tile in two along one of the lines drawn through the centre of the marked pipe hole. Score the outline of each resulting semi-circle with a pencil-type tile cutter. Then use a tile nibbler to cut the hole.

3 Fit the two cut pieces together around the pipe. Grout around the pipe or use a silicone sealant for a water-tight finish.

HELPFUL TIP

If you are filling gaps with cut tiles, butter the back of each tile with adhesive, then press it into place. It is much easier than trying to apply adhesive to a narrow strip of wall.

Tiling around corners

Internal corners

Place all the whole tiles on both walls, then remove the guide battens so that you can cut and fit the tiles in the corner.

1 Measure and cut a tile to fit the width of the gap to be filled. Butter the back of the cut tile with adhesive and press it into place with the cut edge into the corner.

2 When the adhesive has dried, seal the angle between the two walls with a flexible waterproof mastic. This will allow for a little wall movement over time. Use masking tape to mask the joint, apply the mastic, smooth it and peel off the tape once a skin has formed.

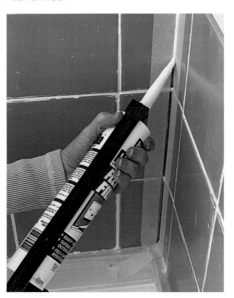

External corners

External corners should, ideally, start with whole tiles on each wall, though this is unlikely to be possible at a window rebate. Joins can be made by butting the tiles, using plastic corner trim or sticking on a strip of timber beading.

Butt joint A simple overlapping butt joint works well if the corner is true and the tiles have glazed edges. Tile the less visible wall first, placing whole tiles flush with the corner. Then tile the other wall, overlapping these tiles to conceal the edges of those on the first wall.

Plastic corner trim
Coloured plastic or chrome corner trims will protect tiles on external corners from damage and give the edge a neat finish. You can use the trim along the edges of tiled door and window recesses as well.

1 Push the perforated base of the trim into the tile adhesive on one corner so that the outer edge of the rounded trim lines up with the faces of the tiles on the adjacent wall.

2 Start tiling the second wall, easing each tile into the corner trim as you place it. Don't push it too hard – you don't want to dislodge the trim. When you have laid all the corner tiles, make sure the trim lines up with the tile faces on both walls.

A window recess

1 Tile the wall as far as the window, cutting tiles to fit. If you have to cut a tile to an L shape, cut a line from the edge to the centre of the tile using a tile saw then score a line at right angles to the cut and snap off the unwanted piece. Use lengths of plastic edging strip designed for external corners to give the edges a neat finish.

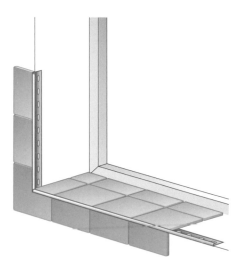

2 Lay the tiles at the bottom of the recess first. Put any cut tiles nearest the window, with cut edges against the frame.

3 Line up the first course of tiles on the side walls with the tiles on the main wall.

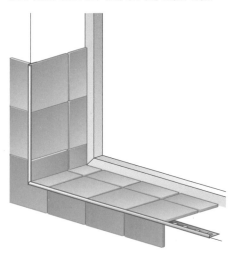

Grouting between tiles

When the tiles have been in place for at least 12 hours, fill the gaps between them with grout. This gives an attractive finish and prevents dirt from collecting in the cracks.

Tools *Pieces of sponge or a squeegee; larger sponge; thin dowel or something similar for finishing; soft dry cloth.*

Materials *Grout (waterproof for kitchens or bathrooms).*

1 If the grout is not ready-mixed, prepare as recommended. With waterproof epoxy-based grout, mix only a little at a time – it sets hard quickly.

2 Press the grout firmly into the gaps between the tiles. Professionals use a rubber-edged squeegee, but if you have never grouted before you may find it easier to use a small piece of sponge.

3 Wipe away any grout that gets onto the surface of the tiles with a clean, damp sponge while the grout is still wet. Wipe away combined adhesive and grout or waterproof grout quickly – these are hard to clean off the tile surface once set.

4 To give the tiling a neat professional finish, run a thin piece of dowelling over each grout line. Or use the cap of a ball-point pen, the blunt end of a pencil or a lolly stick. Wipe surplus off the surface of the tiles as you go.

5 Leave ordinary grout to dry, then polish it off using a clean, dry cloth. Another way to polish tiles effectively is to use a screwed-up ball of newspaper.

Drilling holes through tiles

Many bathroom and kitchen accessories, such as soap dishes, must be screwed to the wall – in which case you may have to drill holes through ceramic tiles.

It's a good idea to make fixings in tiled walls by drilling into grout lines wherever possible, but sometimes drilling through the glaze is unavoidable. Drilling through tiles creates a lot of fine dust, which may stain nearby grouting. To catch the dust, make a simple cardboard tray and stick it to the wall with masking tape or get someone to hold a vacuum-cleaner nozzle near the drill tip as you drill the hole.

Tools *Drill; small masonry bit to make pilot hole and larger one to suit the screw, or sharp spear point bit; chinagraph pencil; screwdriver; possibly steel ruler.*

Materials *Masking tape; wall plugs; screws.*

1 Decide where you want to make the screw fixing and mark its position on the surface of the tile with a chinagraph pencil.

2 Stop the point of the masonry bit from skating over the smooth tile surface by sticking a piece of masking tape over the mark, which should show through it. Re-make the mark on the surface of the tape. If you need to make more than one screw hole, use a strip of tape to cover both hole positions and mark them on the tape.

3 Make a pilot hole with the small masonry bit. Press the tip firmly against the mark on the tape. Check the drill isn't on hammer action, and start at a low speed. Drill slowly and carefully through the glazed surface of the tile. Stop drilling when the bit starts to penetrate the plaster. Using a small bit to do this minimises the risk of cracking the glaze. Repeat the process if necessary to drill a second hole through the other mark on the tape.

4 Switch to the bit that matches the screw size you intend to use. Position its tip in the hole and drill slowly and carefully through the tile and the plaster and well into the masonry.

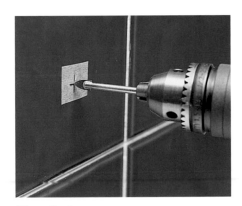

Alternatively You can buy a special ceramic tile bit with a sharp spear point. Its shape is designed to break through the glaze immediately. This minimises the risk of skidding across or cracking the tile. The bits are available in a range of sizes.

HELPFUL TIP

Revive discoloured grout by painting it with a proprietary liquid grout whitener, applied with an artist's brush. Be aware, though, that this is a slow and tedious job.

Restoring a wood floor

Floorboards may be stripped and varnished, stained, painted or limed – before sealing with a hardwearing coating – to create an attractive floor.

Filling holes in floorboards

Use a flexible filler to cover all nail and screw heads – nail heads should be punched below the surface, and screws may need countersinking. If you are painting the floor, the filler colour does not matter; if you are varnishing it, choose a filler slightly lighter in colour than the floor. Once dry, sand filler flush with the floor.

Plugging gaps between boards

There are two ways to deal with gaps: you can fill the gaps, or you can lift and relay the entire floor. Fill narrow gaps with flexible mastic (clear mastic will be almost invisible); wider gaps are best filled with thin lengths of square-edge moulding.

Filling gaps with moulding

1 Plane moulding strips into a slight wedge shape.

2 Apply a little woodworking adhesive before tapping a wedge into a gap, thin edge first.

3 Plane wedges down to floor level when the adhesive has set, then stain to match.

Filling small gaps

Fill gaps between floorboards with a flexible acrylic flooring filler applied with a sealant gun. If you intend to sand and varnish the boards, use a ready-mixed tub filler that can be stained to match the board colour.

Restoring a woodblock floor

Parquet or wood mosaic floor can be rejuvenated by sanding and sealing. It is worth while, as such flooring is expensive and rarely fitted today.

Tools *Dust mask; nail punch and claw hammer; floor sanding machine and edging sander; earmuffs; sanding belts (coarse, medium and fine); edging sander; old chisel; old paintbrush (for adhesive).*

Materials *Flooring varnish or other sealer; latex flooring adhesive.*

Before you start If blocks are missing, a local wood yard may be able to make replacements, you may find them in a reclamation yard or via the Internet (type 'old parquet flooring' into a search engine).

1 Remove any loose blocks and scrape off the adhesive with an old chisel.

2 Spread a layer of latex adhesive into the space in the floor, about 5mm thick, using a filler knife or spatula.

3 Spread a thin layer of adhesive on the back of the block with a paintbrush and immediately put the block in place. Weigh it down by covering with a piece of plastic, a sheet of ply and several bricks, until the adhesive sets.

4 Fill any small gaps with wood filler.

5 Then use the floor sander. Because the grain lies in two directions, the floor must be sanded twice, running the second pass of the machine at right angles to the first.

6 The final sanding, with a very fine belt, will also need to be done in two directions to remove scratch marks.

7 Once the floor is clean and free of dust, apply your chosen finish.

Sanding and varnishing

If floorboards are sound they can be sanded to reveal a beautiful natural floor.

Sanding a floor is hard, dusty, noisy work. On fairly new boards that have not been stained or become too dirty, sanding may not be necessary. Get rid of surface dirt by scrubbing with detergent and hot water. Pay particular attention to removing dirt from nail holes.

Tools *Dust mask; nail punch and claw hammer; floor sanding machine and edging sander (a weekend's hire should be enough for one room); earmuffs; sanding belts and discs (coarse, medium and fine); paint roller and wide paintbrush; fine steel wool.*

Materials *Flooring-grade varnish or other finish.*

Before you start Punch in all the nails in the floor, otherwise they will tear the sanding belts. Any tacks left from previous floor coverings should also be removed. If there are any traces of old polish, remove them with steel wool dipped in white spirit; otherwise the polish will clog up the sanding belt. Wear protective gloves.

1 Start at the edge of the room with your back against the wall. Keep the sander slightly away from the skirting board at the side otherwise you may damage it.

2 It is normal to work along the length of the boards, as sanding across them causes scratches. But if the boards curl up

---

at the edges, make the first runs diagonally across them with a coarse belt. Finish with medium and fine belts along the length of the boards.

3 On a floor where not very much stripping is needed, let the machine go forwards at a slow, steady pace to the far end of the room, lifting up the drum as soon as you reach the skirting board.

4 If the boards are badly marked, wheel the sander backwards to your start point, lower the drum and make a second pass over the first one. Never pull the sander backwards when the drum is rotating or the machine may pull sideways out of control and score the floor surface badly.

5 When the strip looks clean, move on to the next one, and continue to the end of the room. Raise the belt as you change direction or it may damage the boards. You will have started each run about a metre out from the wall behind you. When you have covered the room, turn the machine round and deal with that area.

Sanding the edges

Eventually, you will be left with a narrow border all round the room that the sander cannot reach. This must be stripped with an edging sander. Do not try to use a disc on an electric drill; it is not powerful enough.

1 Use the edging sander all round the edges of the room, taking care not to damage the paint on the skirting boards.

2 When the sanding is finished, vacuum-clean the floor to get rid of all the wood dust. Do not damp the floor as the water may leave marks.

3 Finally, mop the floor with a clean, dry, lint-free cloth. Be sure to shake it frequently outdoors to get rid of the last particles.

Applying varnish

The quickest way of sealing a newly stripped floor is to use a paint roller to apply the varnish. Thin the first coat as recommended on the container to aid penetration, and apply full-strength for the second and third coats. Use a power sander fitted with fine abrasive paper to sand the surface lightly between coats, and wipe it with a damp cloth to remove dust before re-coating it.

1 Apply the varnish with criss-cross passes of the roller, then finish off by running it parallel with the boards.

2 Use a paintbrush to finish the floor edges and to cut in round obstacles such as central heating pipes.

RE-LAYING FLOORBOARDS

If you decide to re-lay the floorboards, you need to fit the first board tight to the wall, and butt each board up against the previous one using a tool called a floor cramp, which can be hired.

Lifting and replacing a floorboard

You may need to lift a floorboard in order to access pipes or cables beneath the floor for repairs.

Tools *Thin-bladed knife; drill and twist drill bits; jigsaw; bolster chisel; hammer; screwdriver. Also for tongue-and-groove boards: circular saw (or panel saw or flooring saw).*

Materials *50 or 75mm floorboard nails; 75mm No. 8 screws; pieces of timber about 40mm square and 100mm longer than the width of the boards.*

Before you start First find out whether the boards are tongue-and-groove or square edge by poking a thin-bladed knife between them. If they are square edge, the blade will pass right through.

Removing a square-edge board

Before lifting the board, you must cut across it at each end just before it meets a joist. Lines of nails indicate joist centres.

1 Drill a 10mm starting hole near the edge of the board you want to remove and complete the cut across it with a jigsaw.

2 Starting at one end, prise out fixing nails by levering up the board with a bolster chisel.

3 Once you have loosened one or two sets of nails, push the handle of a hammer under the board as far from the loose end as possible, and try to prise the board up. This sends a shock wave along the whole length, loosening nails farther along, which you can then remove.

4 Push the hammer farther forward, and repeat the process, until the board is free.

How to remove tongues

On tongue-and-groove boards, the tongues on each side of the board must be removed. If adjoining boards are to be lifted, only the tongues at the outer edges of the group need cutting.

1 Adjust the depth of cut on a circular saw so that the blade just protrudes below the underside of the tongue. Since floorboards are usually 19mm thick, the underside of the tongue will be about 13mm below the surface. This will avoid pipes and cables. If you do not have a circular saw, use a panel or flooring saw. Cut at a shallow angle.

2 Place the blade between the boards, switch on the power, and move the saw along the length of board.

---

3 With the tongues removed you should be able to see the joists between the boards. Remove the board in the same way as a square-edge board.

Replacing the board

Use new nails and proper floorboard brads. You will not be able to nail the board to a joist at its ends as it has been sawn off before the joists.

1 Screw a short batten to the side of each joist, its top edge jammed hard up against the underside of adjacent floorboards still in position. Nail the board to the batten.

Alternatively If you have old ceilings, it may be wise to screw the boards down. Vibration from heavy hammering can cause ceiling damage. Screws are also useful if access may be needed to pipes or cables beneath the floor in future.

How to hang a front or back door

When buying a new door, measure the height and width of the frame and get a door that is either the right size or slightly too big. An exterior door is heavy, so get someone to help you if you can.

Panelled doors can have up to 20mm removed all round to fit, but most flush doors should have no more than about 10mm planed away, otherwise they may be seriously weakened.

Flush doors contain wooden blocks for fitting hinges and locks; their positions are marked on the edges of the door. When fitting the hinges and locks, note where the blocks are as they will affect the way round that the door is placed in the frame. If you want to reverse the face of the door, most are reversible top to bottom.

You will need three butt hinges – either 75mm or 100mm long. The job will be simpler if you choose a size to fit the existing hinge recesses on the frame.

If a flush door is being fitted, buy pressed-steel cranked butt hinges. A panelled door, which is heavier, requires cast butt hinges.

Tools *Pencil; tape measure; try square; marking gauge; 19mm or 25mm chisel; mallet; plane; panel or tenon saw; trimming knife; drill and twist bits; screwdriver; folding workbench.*

Materials *Exterior door; three hinges; screws to fit (check that the heads fit fully into the countersunk holes on the hinge).*

REMOVING STUBBORN SCREWS

When you remove your old door, the hinge screws may be difficult to get out. Scrape off any paint, particularly out of the slots. If a screw still will not shift, put a screwdriver in the slot and hit it with a mallet.

---

1 Remove the old door carefully, without damaging the hinge recesses on the frame. Put pieces of wood under the door to take the weight while you remove the screws, and get someone to hold it.

2 New panelled doors are sometimes protected with strips of timber or cork pads at the edges; remove these by prising them off with a broad scraper blade.

Getting the fit right

1 Hold the door against the frame to mark it for trimming. A glass-panelled door is usually fitted with the putty on the outside and decorative wood beading on the inside.

2 When the door is centrally positioned, get someone to steady it and put wedges underneath to hold it at the correct height.

3 Lightly mark the face with a soft pencil to give the correct gap round the perimeter. A panelled door should have a gap of 3mm all round to allow the wood to swell in wet weather. A flush door should have a gap of 2mm. If the frame is straight you may not have to trim all the edges of the door. However, if the frame is out of true, or if there is a fair amount of trimming to do, it will be necessary to trim all round.

4 If there is more than about 5mm of wood to remove, lay the door flat on boxes or trestles and saw it close to the trimming line, then finish off with a plane.

5 For planing, hold the door on its edge in the jaws of a folding adjustable workbench. Protect the bottom edge on scrap timber and then plane the top edge down to the pencilled trimming line.

6 Plane the long edges of the door in the direction of the grain. The shavings will be removed smoothly, whereas if you plane against the grain the blade will tend to dig into the wood.

7 Plane the top and bottom edges of the door from each side towards the centre. This will avoid splitting wood at the edge of the stiles where you will be planing across the grain.

8 Stand the door in the frame on wedges and check there is the right gap all round.

9 When the fit is correct, plane a slight slope on the edges of both door stiles towards the doorstop on the frame. This will ensure that the door will close easily without binding against the frame.

Hanging the door

1 Hold the door in the frame to mark the hinge positions. If the hinge recesses in the frame are already cut to the right size, mark the top and bottom of the recesses on the edge of the door. If not, increase the size with a chisel as explained below, and then mark the top and bottom of the hinge positions on the door.

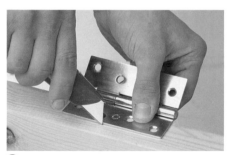

2 Hold the hinge in place on the door and mark round the edge of each hinge flap with a trimming knife. With a cranked butt hinge the whole knuckle of the hinge should project from the face of the door and from the frame. With a cast butt hinge the centre of the knuckle should be in line with the face of the door and frame.

3 Mark the thickness of the flap on the door face with a marking gauge.

4 Cut around the perimeter of the hinge recess with a sharp chisel. Then make a series of cuts about 5mm apart across the grain of the wood, and carefully pare away the waste.

5 Screw the hinge flaps into the recesses in the door, putting only one screw in each hinge for the time being.

6 Hold the door open on wedges and screw the hinges to the frame – again using one screw each. Each screw head should lie flush with the surface of the hinge flap.

If the screw heads protrude, they will bind and prevent the door from closing. You can either deepen the countersinks in the hinge with a high-speed-steel twist bit in a power drill, or else you could buy screws one gauge size smaller.

If the screws do not tighten into the frame, glue pieces of dowel in the old screw holes and drill new ones.

7 Check that the door swings open and shut easily. If it does not close properly, the hinge positions may have to be adjusted.

8 When the door moves correctly, insert the remaining hinge screws.

Patching damaged plaster

Large cracks, holes or crumbling areas of plaster can generally be repaired quickly and cheaply with plaster.

Damage caused by damp Do not repair damage caused by damp until the cause has been remedied. If large cracks reopen after repair, get the advice of a builder or surveyor as the cracks may be caused by structural movement of the building.

Using ready-mixed plaster

Tools *Cold chisel; club hammer; hand brush; filling knife or plasterer's trowel. Possibly also fine abrasive paper or power sander; face mask and safety goggles; large paintbrush; plastic spreader (supplied with skim-coat container).*

Materials *Ready-mixed plaster. Possibly ready-mixed skim-coat plaster.*

1 Chip away loose or crumbling plaster with a cold chisel until you reach a firm surface all round.

2 Brush away dust and debris. If bricks or building blocks are exposed, dampen the areas with water.

3 Stir the plaster and apply it to the wall with a filling knife or plasterer's trowel held at an angle.

4 Build up deep areas in layers – applied up to 50mm deep in cavities. Allow each layer to stiffen before applying the next.

5 If the surface is to be papered, fill the undercoat to the top of the damaged area. When it is thoroughly dry, smooth it with fine abrasive paper or a power sander. Wear a mask and goggles to protect you from dust.

Alternatively If the surface is to be painted, fill the top 3mm of the area with a coat of skim plaster to give a smooth finish. Apply it with a large brush, in upward strokes, then spread it with light strokes. When it begins to dry, smooth it with the plastic spreader supplied.

USING ONE-COAT PLASTER

Mix the plaster according to the instructions on the packet – generally up to about 500ml cold water per 1kg of powder – until it is a smooth paste that is just stiff enough to use. Apply it in the same way as ordinary plaster and finish in the same way.

Repairing holes in plasterboard

Small holes in plasterboard can be repaired in the same way as in plaster, but first you will need to fit a backing piece to block the cavity.

To repair a larger area, cut the plasterboard back to expose a timber stud on either side. Fit a cross timber, or noggin, at the top and bottom of the gap and nail a replacement plasterboard panel in place. Sand the edges and fill with joint compound.

Tools *Pencil and ruler; trimming knife; drill and twist bit; padsaw or mini hacksaw; filling knife; sanding block; scissors; length of wood.*

Materials *A plasterboard offcut or a piece of MDF; piece of string 150–200mm long; a long nail or wood sliver; interior or plaster filler or coving adhesive.*

1 Draw a neat square around the damaged area, and drill holes at the corners so that you can get the blade of your padsaw in. Cut along the lines to create a neat, straight sided hole.

2 Cut a backing piece from a plasterboard or MDF offcut. It should be narrow enough to go through the hole, but long enough to overlap the hole by about 25mm at the top and bottom.

3 Bore a hole in the middle of the backing piece and thread the length of string through it.

4 Knot a nail or a sliver of wood to one end of the string to anchor it against the back of the offcut. Make sure you have the ivory side (which will be covered with plaster filler) as the front. Make a loop in the front end of the string so that it is easy to hold.

5 Apply coving adhesive or filler to the front (the ivory side) of the backing piece.

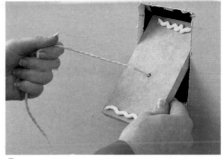

6 Guide the coated backing piece through the hole, then use the string to pull it into position against the back of the hole.

7 The patch should stick fairly quickly. Cut off the string when you are sure it has stuck firmly.

8 Use quick-setting filler to cover the patch, filling the hole to about half its depth. When it has dried, put in another layer, leaving it slightly proud.

9 With a length of wood, skim off the excess filler, leaving a smooth surface level with the surrounding area.

10 When the filler has dried, smooth the surface with a sanding block or sheet of fine abrasive paper round a wooden block.

Tools for plumbing

You will have most of the basic tools needed for plumbing in your toolkit. For more specialist jobs, tools and equipment can be bought or hired.

Pipe wrenches For gripping pipes, circular fittings or hexagonal nuts that have been rounded off at the edges. Two wrenches are needed for some jobs. Some pipe wrenches, such as Footprint wrenches, are operated by squeezing the handles together. The Stillson type has an adjuster nut for altering the jaw size. Useful sizes are 250mm and 360mm, with jaw openings up to 25mm and 38mm. For a cistern-retaining nut you may need a wrench or an adjustable spanner that will open to 60mm.

When using a wrench, always push or pull in the direction of the jaw opening. Pad the jaws with cloth if they are likely to damage the fitting – if it is plastic, for example.

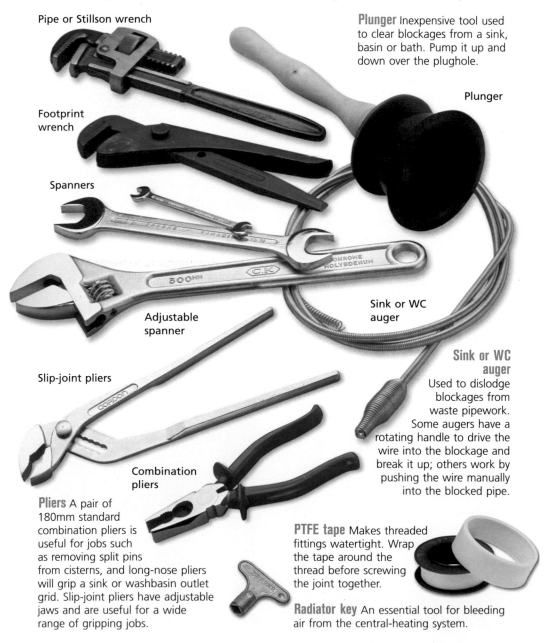

Pipe or Stillson wrench

Footprint wrench

Spanners

Adjustable spanner

Slip-joint pliers

Combination pliers

Plunger Inexpensive tool used to clear blockages from a sink, basin or bath. Pump it up and down over the plughole.

Plunger

Sink or WC auger

Sink or WC auger Used to dislodge blockages from waste pipework. Some augers have a rotating handle to drive the wire into the blockage and break it up; others work by pushing the wire manually into the blocked pipe.

Pliers A pair of 180mm standard combination pliers is useful for jobs such as removing split pins from cisterns, and long-nose pliers will grip a sink or washbasin outlet grid. Slip-joint pliers have adjustable jaws and are useful for a wide range of gripping jobs.

PTFE tape Makes threaded fittings watertight. Wrap the tape around the thread before screwing the joint together.

Radiator key An essential tool for bleeding air from the central-heating system.

Cutting off the water supply

In many homes, only the kitchen tap is fed from the rising main; others are fed from the cold water cistern.

Taps fed from the cistern

1 To isolate a hot or cold tap supplied from the cistern, turn off the gatevalve on the supply pipe from the cistern. If a service valve is fitted in the pipe to the tap (see below), turn it off with a screwdriver.

2 Turn on the tap until the water has stopped flowing.

Alternatively If there is no gatevalve or service valve on the pipe, you will have to drain the cistern.

SERVICE VALVES

Draining down the system provides a good opportunity to fit service valves on the pipes supplying every tap and WC cistern ballvalve. Having done this, you will be able to isolate any tap or ballvalve for repair or replacement without having to drain the entire system.

Draining the cistern

1 Tie the ballvalve arm to a piece of wood laid across the cistern (see page 116). This stops the flow from the mains.

2 Turn on the bathroom cold taps until the water stops flowing, then turn on the hot taps – very little water will flow from them. (You need not turn off the boiler.)

Taps fed from the rising main

Turn off the main indoor stoptap, then turn on the mains-fed tap until the water stops.

Draining the rising main

You may want to drain the rising main to take a branch pipe from it or to repair the main stoptap. If there is a drain valve above the stoptap, fit a short piece of hose to its outlet and open it with a drain valve key or pliers. Catch the water, usually only a litre or two, in a bucket.

Turning off the outdoor stoptap

You may need to turn off the outdoor stoptap if the indoor one is broken, jammed or has a leak from the spindle. Stoptap keys can be bought from plumbers' merchants, but first check the type needed – the tap may have a crutch handle or a square spindle.

Alternatively If you have no stoptap key, make your own. Take a piece of strong wood about 1m long and in one end cut a V-shaped slot about 25mm wide at the opening and 75mm deep. Securely fix a piece of wood as a cross-bar handle at the other end. Slip the slot over the stoptap handle to turn it. This tool will not turn a stoptap with a square spindle.

1 Locate the stoptap, which is under a cover, about 100mm across, just inside or just outside the boundary of your property. If you cannot find the outdoor stoptap, call your water supply company.

2 Raise the cover. This may be difficult if it has not been raised for some time.

3 Insert the stoptap key into the guard pipe and engage the stoptap handle at the bottom. Turn it clockwise.

Draining down the system

Central-heating systems sometimes have to be drained down – to repair a leak, for example. The following method is for an open-vented system, the most common type.

1 Switch off the boiler at the programmer or time switch.

2 Turn off the gas, either at the isolating gas cock near the boiler or by the gas meter. Make sure that the fire in a solid-fuel boiler is out and that the boiler is cold. There is no need to turn off the oil supply in an oil-fired system.

3 Shut off the water supply to the feed-and-expansion cistern. There should be a separate stoptap for this on the branch pipe from the rising main connected to the cistern's ballvalve.

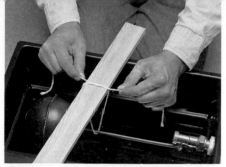

4 If there is no separate stoptap, or it is jammed and cannot be turned, stop the water flow into the cistern by tying up the ballvalve to a piece of wood laid across the top of the cistern.

5 Locate the drain valve, which may be near the bottom of the boiler. There may be more than one drainage point on the system. Clip a garden hose onto the outlet and run the hose to a drain outside.

6 Locate all the points at which air is vented from the central heating system. There will be radiator vents, a vent on the primary flow near the hot water cylinder in fully pumped systems, and manual or automatic vents in the loft if circulating pipes run there. There could be additional vents at other points as well.

7 Open the drain valve with a spanner or pliers, turning counter-clockwise. Water will then start to flow out of the hose at a fairly slow rate.

8 Start opening the venting points at the top of the system. This will greatly speed up the flow from the drain valve. As the water level drops further, open the lower venting points until they are all open.

Refilling the system

1 Close all the drain valves and all the air vents in the system. Then check that all work on the system is finished.

2 Turn on the stoptap to the header tank, or untie the ballvalve, to let water back in.

3 Open one of the lowest air vents until water starts to flow out, then close it. Repeat with the lower air vents until the bottom of the central-heating system is full of water. Repeat with the upper vents.

4 Make sure that the ballvalve to the header tank has closed. The water level in the cistern should be just high enough to float the ball. The rest of the cistern space is to take up the expansion of the water in the system as it heats up.

5 If the water level is too high, close off the mains water supply to the cistern and open the drain valve to let some out. Adjust the arm on the ballvalve so that it closes the valve at the correct water level. Check that the cistern's lid and insulating jacket are in place.

6 Switch on the electricity and turn on the gas. Re-light the pilot light in a gas boiler. Turn on the system at the programmer or timeswitch. Turn up the room thermostat.

7 Re-light the boiler, following the manufacturer's instructions.

8 As the system heats up, more venting will be necessary in order to release air driven off from the water. Minor venting will be required for a few days.

9 Check for leaks again. Then remove the hose from the drain valve and make sure the valve is watertight. If it is leaking, drain the system again and remove the spindle. Remove the washer on the end of the spindle and replace it with a new one. Use fibre rather than a rubber one, which can bake on and disintegrate.

Dealing with a blocked sink

Proprietary cleaning products can free a sink that is slow to empty, but if the water is not draining away at all, you will need the help of a plunger.

Tools *Possibly a length of wire; sink-waste plunger; sink auger or a length of expanding curtain wire; bucket.*

Materials *Possibly caustic soda or proprietary chemical or enzyme cleaner; petroleum jelly.*

1 Place the sink plunger cup squarely over the plug hole.

2 Stuff a damp cloth firmly into the overflow and hold it there. This stops air escaping through the hole and dissipating the force you build up by plunging.

3 Pump the plunger sharply up and down. If the blockage does not clear, repeat.

4 If plunging fails, replace the sink plug. Put a bucket under the sink and disconnect the trap. Wash it out thoroughly.

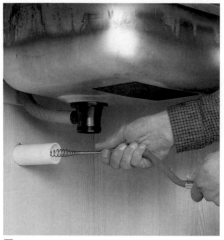

5 If the obstruction is not in the trap, try using a plumber's snake. It is a spiral device that can be hired or bought. Disconnect the blocked pipe from its trap and feed the wire into it. Then turn the handle to rotate the spiral. This drives its cutting head into the blockage and breaks it up.

Alternatively If you have a vacuum cleaner that is designed to cope with liquids, you can use it to try to dislodge a blockage in a sink trap. Press a cloth over the overflow in the sink. Then place the suction tube of the vacuum over the plughole and switch on. This will probably loosen the blockage sufficiently to allow it to be carried away by the water flow through the trap.

Alternatively If you have poured fat into the sink and it has hardened, try warming the pipe with a hair dryer, to melt the grease. Flush plenty of hot water after it.

CLEARING THE PIPES

If a sink is slow to empty, smear petroleum jelly on the rim of the plug hole to protect it, and then apply proprietary chemical or enzyme cleaner according to the manufacturer's instructions.

Washing machines and dishwashers are often plumbed in to feed the under-sink waste trap. Alternatively, they may join the main waste pipe at a T-junction away from the sink. If all your appliances feed into the one trap, you may need to disconnect all the pipes in turn and then clean each one to clear a blockage.

Joining pipes

Compression and speedfit joints are the most reliable way for DIY plumbers to join pipes together, whether they are copper, plastic or uPVC.

Preparing the pipe ends

Before two pipe lengths of any material can be joined, the ends must be cut square and left smooth. Copper pipe needs careful cutting and finishing to ensure watertight joints. You can cut plastic pipes with special shears or with a sharp craft knife.

Tools *Pipe cutter or hacksaw; half-round file. Possibly also vice or portable workbench.*

1 Cut the pipe ends square using a pipe cutter or hacksaw. Holding the pipe in a vice helps to ensure a square cut.

2 Smooth away burrs inside the cut ends with the reamer on the pipe cutter. Use a file to smooth the end and the outside of the pipe.

Making a compression joint

A strong, easy method of joining copper and plastic pipes is to use compression joints, which are made watertight with nuts and sealing rings called olives inside the joint. Tightening the nuts correctly is critical: make them too tight or too loose and the joint will leak.

Tools *Two adjustable spanners (with jaw openings up to 38mm wide for fittings on 28mm piping); or, if you have any that fit, two open-ended spanners – capnut sizes on different makes of fittings vary.*

Materials *Compression fitting.*

1 Unscrew and remove one capnut from the fitting. If the olive has two sloping faces rather than a convex one, note which way round it is fitted, then remove it as well.

2 Take one pipe and slide the capnut over it, then the olive. Make sure the olive is the same way round as it was in the fitting if it has two sloping faces. Push the pipe into one end of the fitting up to the internal pipe stop. Then slide the olive and nut up to the fitting and hand-tighten the capnut.

3 Hold the body of the fitting securely with one spanner while you give the capnut one and a quarter turns with the other. Do not overtighten it further. Fit pipes into other openings of the fitting in the same way.

Making a Speedfit joint

This is a simple method that can be used to join both copper and plastic pipes. The only tools needed are those used to cut and smooth the pipe ends.

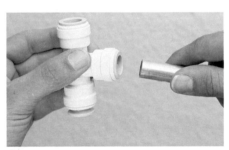

1 Take one of the pipe ends and push it into the fitting until it clicks into the toothed ring.

2 Fit piping into the other end(s) of the fitting in the same way.

Making a push-fit joint for waste pipes

Push-fit or ring-seal joints must be used to connect polypropylene waste pipes, which cannot be solvent-welded. Joints can be re-used with a new seal.

Tools *Hacksaw; sharp knife; clean rag; newspaper; adhesive tape; pencil.*

Materials *Push-fit joint; silicone grease.*

1 Wrap a sheet of newspaper round the pipe as a saw guide. Cut the pipe square with a hacksaw.

2 Use a sharp knife to remove fine shavings of polypropylene and rough edges.

3 Wipe dust from inside the fitting and the outside of the pipe.

4 On a locking-ring connector, loosen the locking ring.

Sealing ring —
Locking ring —

5 Make sure that the sealing ring is properly in place, with any taper pointing inwards. If necessary, remove the nut to check.

6 Lubricate the end of the pipe with silicone grease.

7 Push the pipe into the socket as far as the stop – a slight inner ridge about 25mm from the end. This allows a gap of about 10mm at the pipe end for heat expansion.

8 Tighten the locking ring.

Making a solvent-welded joint

Because solvent-welded joints are neat they are suitable for exposed MuPVC pipework. However, they are permanent and should only be used where they will not need to be disturbed. Push-fit connections are used at traps, where the joint may need to be undone occasionally.

Tools *Hacksaw; half-round file; cloth.*

Materials *Solvent-weld cement; appropriate connector; appropriate pipe.*

1 Cut the pipes to the required length with a hacksaw, remove the burrs inside and out with a half-round file, and wipe thoroughly with a clean cloth.

2 Apply solvent-weld cement around the end of the pipe and push it into the joint.

3 Wipe off excess cement with the cloth and allow the joint to dry before moving on to the next joint.

Bending copper pipe

To make a new length of pipe connect precisely with another pipe or plumbing fitting, you may need to bend it. Never try to bend rigid copper pipe by hand without a spring to support the pipe walls – the pipe will kink at the bend.

Tools *Bending springs of the required diameter (15mm or 22mm); or pipe-bending machine with pipe formers and guide blocks; screwdriver; length of string.*

Materials *Petroleum jelly.*

1 If the pipe is longer than the spring, tie string to the spring end.

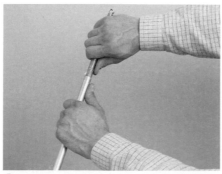

2 Grease the spring well with petroleum jelly and push it into the pipe.

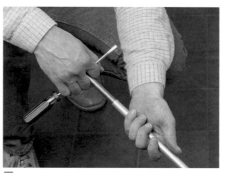

3 Bend the pipe across your knee with gentle hand pressure to the required angle.

4 Overbend the pipe a little more, then ease it gently back again. This action helps to free the spring and makes it easier to withdraw.

5 Insert a screwdriver blade through the spring loop. Twist the spring to reduce its diameter, then pull it out.

Alternatively Bend copper pipes with a machine. Clamp the pipe against the correct-sized semicircular former. Place the guide block of the correct diameter between the pipe and the movable handle. Squeeze the handles together until the pipe is curved to the required angle round the semicircular former.

Tools for wiring work

Many of the jobs involved in wiring are non-electrical in nature – lifting floorboards, say. But for the electrical work, some special tools are essential.

Torch Choose one with a sturdy stand or clip-on fitting. A powerful torch will light up work under floors and in lofts. Ideally, choose a torch with a rechargeable battery. If not, keep a supply of spare batteries handy.

Wire cutters A pair of 125mm or 150mm wire cutters will cut cable and flex, and trim cores to length.

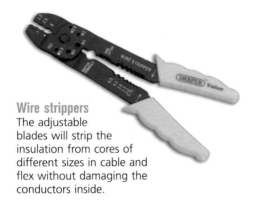

Wire strippers The adjustable blades will strip the insulation from cores of different sizes in cable and flex without damaging the conductors inside.

Circuit continuity tester With a simple battery-powered tester you can check the continuity of circuits and whether a socket outlet is on a ring main circuit or on a spur.

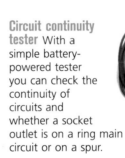

Pliers A pair of 150mm electrician's pliers is useful for twisting cable conductor cores together prior to insertion into terminals. The cutting jaws can also be used for cutting cable and flex.

Tester screwdriver An insulated screwdriver with a 3mm blade is used for tightening terminal screws in plugs and other wiring accessories. A bulb in the handle lights up if the tip touches a live terminal or conductor.

Insulated screwdriver Larger with an insulating sleeve on the shaft. It is useful for undoing and tightening plug screws and screws fixing accessory faceplates to their mounting boxes.

Knife A sharp knife will cut through thick cable sheath and flex sheath.

Choosing the right fuse

Always use the correct fuse for the job in hand. NEVER use any other metallic object or material in place of a blown fuse in order to restore power to a circuit or appliance. Doing so would remove the

protection the fuse provides, and could allow an electrical fire to start or result in someone receiving a potentially fatal electric shock.

Fuse wires

If your consumer unit has rewirable fuses, use 5amp wire for a lighting circuit, 15amp wire for an immersion heater circuit, and 30amp wire for a ring main circuit or a circuit to a cooker rated at up to 12kW.

Cartridge fuses

5A Use for a lighting circuit

15A Use for a storage heater or immersion heater circuit.

20A Use for a 20amp radial power circuit.

30A Use for a ring main circuit or a 30amp radial power circuit.

45A Use for a cooker or shower circuit.

Choosing flexes

Most flex is round in cross-section and has a white PVC outer sheath that contains colour-coded insulated conductors. The live conductor is brown, the neutral blue and the earth green-and-yellow. Each conductor (called a core) is a bundle of thin wires, which is why it is so flexible. The thicker the core, the more strands it has and the more current it can carry.

Ordinary PVC-sheathed flex will withstand temperatures of up to 60°C; heat-resistant rubber-sheathed flex up to 85°C. Non-kink flex has a rubber sheath with an outer cover of braided fabric. Flex with an orange sheath is used out of doors to make it easy to see.

Metal light fittings and most appliances need three-core flex. Two-core flex with no earth core is used on double-insulated power tools and appliances (marked ▣), and for wiring non-metallic light fittings.

Key to flex colours
L – Live (brown)
E – Earth (green and yellow)
N – Neutral (blue)

2-core flex For non-metallic light-fittings and double-insulated appliances. Available with flat or round PVC sheath. Use 0.5mm² for up to 700W with a lampshade weight of 2kg; 0.75mm² for up to 1.4kW and 3kg; and 1mm² for up to 2.3kW and lampshade weight of 5kg.

3-core flex Used for all other appliances and for metallic light fittings and pendant lampholders requiring earthing. Has a round PVC sheath. Use 0.75mm² flex for up to 1.4kW; 1mm² for up to 2.3kW; 1.25mm² for up to 2.9kW; 1.5mm² for up to 3.6kW. Use 1.5mm² heat-resisting flex for immersion heaters.

3-core braided flex Used for portable appliances, such as irons, toasters and room heaters, with hot parts that could damage PVC-sheathed flex. Use sizes as for 3-core PVC flex.

3-core curly flex Useful for worktop appliances such as kettles, to keep flex safe and tidy. Use sizes as for 3-core flex.

Preparing flex for connection

The cores inside flex must be exposed before they can be connected to the terminals of a plug, appliance or ceiling rose.

Tools *Sharp knife; wire cutters and strippers; pliers.*

Materials *Flex. Possibly also PVC insulating tape or a rubber sleeve.*

Stripping the outer sheath

Most flex has an outer sheath of tough PVC. Remove enough to make sure that the cores can reach the terminals easily or they may be pulled out. For most connections you need to remove about 40mm of the sheath. Take care not to cut or nick the insulation on the cores as you cut the outer sheath.

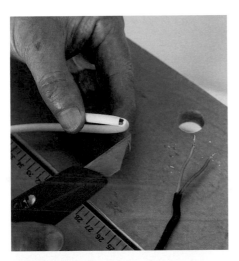

Bend the flex over and cut the sheath lightly with a sharp knife. The tension at the fold will open up a split halfway round the sheath. Fold the flex the other way and repeat. Then pull off the unwanted length of sheath.

Cutting and stripping the cores

1 Cut the individual cores to the right length to reach their terminals.

2 Set the wire strippers to match the thickness of the cores you are stripping. The core should just be able to slide out of the opening in the tool.

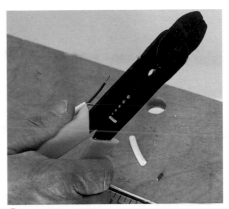

3 Press the handles together to cut the core insulation about 15mm from the tip. Rotate the strippers half a turn and pull them towards the tip of the core. The insulation will slide off.

4 Twist the strands of wire together.

Alternatively If you are preparing very thin flex for connection, strip off 30mm of insulation from each core, rather than 15mm. Twist the wire strands together, then fold the bare core over on itself in a tight U-shape. This makes it easier to insert into the terminal and provides a better electrical contact.

Fabric-covered flex

The outer cover of braided fabric on non-kink flex is likely to fray where it is cut. Wrap a strip of PVC insulating tape two or three times round the cut end of the fabric to seal down the loose threads.

Alternatively Cover the cut with a purpose–made rubber sleeve. This will be held by the cord grip of the plug. Remember to put it on before inserting the flex in the plug.

Wiring new flex

Whether you are extending a flex or replacing a lampholder or power socket, the principles of making safe electrical connections are the same as those shown here for changing a plug.

Tools *Insulated screwdrivers; sharp knife; wire cutters and strippers; pliers.*

1 Unscrew the cover of the new plug and remove it.

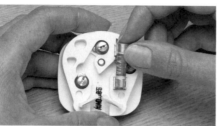

2 Prise out the cartridge fuse if necessary to reveal the terminal. Loosen the screw-down bar that secures the flex if there is one. Plastic jaws grip the flex in some plugs.

3 If you are replacing a hand-wired plug, remove its cover and loosen the terminal screws to release the flex cores from their terminals. Release the flex from the flex grip. Inspect the bare cores. If they appear damaged, cut them off and strip off some core insulation to expose undamaged wires.

4 If you are replacing a factory-fitted plug, cut through the flex close to the plug body. Prepare the end of the cut flex. For some plugs all the cores have to be the same length, for others they have to be different lengths. Check that the prepared cores are long enough to reach their terminals with the flex sheath held in the flex grip.

5 Tough rubber plugs designed for use on power tools have a hole in the plug cover through which the flex passes before being connected to the plug terminals.

6 Connect each flex core to its correct terminal. The **BR**own (live) core goes to the **B**ottom **R**ight terminal, the **BL**ue (neutral) core to the **B**ottom **L**eft terminal, and the earth core in three-core flex (green-and-yellow) to the top terminal.

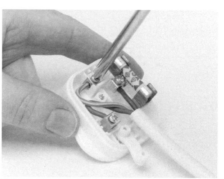

7 With pillar-type terminals, loosen the terminal screw and insert the bare end of the core in the hole. Tighten the screw to trap it in place. Plugs with this type of terminal often have loose pins; remove these from the plug first if it makes connecting the cores easier.

Alternatively With screw-down stud terminals, remove the stud and wind the bare end of the core clockwise round the threaded peg. Screw the stud down to trap the wires in place.

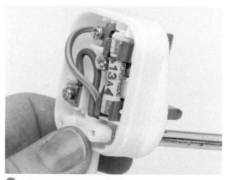

8 Arrange the cores in their channels in the plug body and place the flex sheath in the cord grip. If the plug has nylon jaws, press the flex in between them. If it has a screw-down bar, undo one screw, position the flex in the grip, swing the bar back over it and screw it down securely. Fit the fuse.

9 Replace the plug cover and make sure that it is firmly screwed together.

Acknowledgments

All images in this book are copyright of the Reader's Digest Association Limited, with the exception of those in the following list.

The position of photographs and illustrations on each page is indicated by letters after the page number:
T = Top; **B** = Bottom; **L** = Left; **R** = Right; **C** = Centre

The majority of images in this book are © Reader's Digest and were previously published in Reader's Digest *DIY Manual*

2 iStockphoto.com/Jim Jurica
8–9 Shutterstock, Inc./Elnur
26–27 Shutterstock, Inc./Bella Media
70–71 Shutterstock, Inc./J. Helgason

80, 83, 86T, 88TR & BR, 95TR, CR, & BL, 101 GE Fabbri Limited
104–105 Shutterstock, Inc./Tom Davison
113 GE Fabbri Limited

Reader's Digest *DIY Tools and Techniques* is based on material in Reader's Digest *DIY Manual*, published by The Reader's Digest Association Limited, London.

First Edition Copyright © 2008
The Reader's Digest Association Limited,
11 Westferry Circus, Canary Wharf,
London E14 4HE
www.readersdigest.co.uk

Editor Alison Candlin
Art Editors Keith Miller, Jane McKenna
Assistant Editor Diane Cross
Editorial Consultant Mike Lawrence
Proofreader Ron Pankhurst
Indexer Marie Lorimer

Reader's Digest General Books
Editorial Director Julian Browne
Art Director Anne-Marie Bulat
Managing Editor Nina Hathway
Head of Book Development Sarah Bloxham
Picture Resource Manager Sarah Stewart-Richardson
Pre-press Account Managers Penelope Grose and Dean Russell
Production Controller Sandra Fuller
Product Production Manager Claudette Bramble

Origination Colour Systems Limited, London
Printed and bound in China by CT Printing

The contents of this book are believed to be accurate at the time of printing. However the publisher accepts no responsibility or liability for any work carried out in the absence of professional advice.

We are committed both to the quality of our products and the service we provide to our customers. We value your comments, so please do contact us on 08705 113366, or via our website at www.readersdigest.co.uk

If you have any comments about the content of our books, email us at gbeditorial@readersdigest.co.uk

ISBN 978 0 276 44301 5
BOOK CODE 400-371 UP0000-1
ORACLE CODE 250011972H.00.24